TIGER WOODS

TIGER WOODS

William C. Durbin

CHELSEA HOUSE PUBLISHERS
Philadelphia

To my son Reid, who hits it
farther and straighter than I
—William C. Durbin

Chelsea House Publishers

Editor-in-Chief	Stephen Reginald
Managing Editor	James D. Gallagher
Production Manager	Pamela Loos
Art Director	Sara Davis
Photo Editor	Judy Hasday
Senior Production Editor	Lisa Chippendale

Staff for TIGER WOODS

Senior Editor	James D. Gallagher
Editorial Assistant	Anne Hill
Associate Art Director	Takeshi Takahashi
Designer	Keith Trego
Picture Researcher	Sandy Jones
Cover Illustrator	Bradford Brown

The Chelsea House World Wide Web site address is
http://www.chelseahouse.com

5 7 9 8 6 4

Durbin, William C.
  Tiger Woods/ William C. Durbin
    p. cm. — (Black Americans of Achievement)
  Includes bibliographical references (p.) and index
Summary: Examines the life and golf career of the young man who
racked up numerous tournament victories and became celebrated
in the media.
ISBN 0-7910-4651-6
       0-7910-4687-7 (pbk.)
1. Woods, Tiger—Juvenile literature. 2. Golfers—United States—
Biography—Juvenile literature. 3. Racially mixed people—United
States—Biography—Juvenile literature. [1. Woods, Tiger. 2.
Golfers. 3. Racially mixed people—Biography.] I. Title. II. Series.
GV964.W66D87   1998
796.352'092—dc21
[B]   97-40746
                                    CIP
                                    AC

CONTENTS

————— ❧ —————

BLACK AMERICANS OF ACHIEVEMENT

HENRY AARON
baseball great

KAREEM ABDUL-JABBAR
basketball great

MUHAMMAD ALI
heavyweight champion

RICHARD ALLEN
religious leader and social activist

MAYA ANGELOU
author

LOUIS ARMSTRONG
musician

ARTHUR ASHE
tennis great

JOSEPHINE BAKER
entertainer

TYRA BANKS
model

BENJAMIN BANNEKER
scientist and mathematician

COUNT BASIE
bandleader and composer

ANGELA BASSETT
actress

ROMARE BEARDEN
artist

HALLE BERRY
actress

MARY MCLEOD BETHUNE
educator

GEORGE WASHINGTON
CARVER
botanist

JOHNNIE COCHRAN
lawyer

BILL COSBY
entertainer

MILES DAVIS
musician

FREDERICK DOUGLASS
abolitionist editor

CHARLES DREW
physician

PAUL LAURENCE DUNBAR
poet

DUKE ELLINGTON
bandleader and composer

RALPH ELLISON
author

JULIUS ERVING
basketball great

LOUIS FARRAKHAN
political activist

ELLA FITZGERALD
singer

ARETHA FRANKLIN
entertainer

MORGAN FREEMAN
actor

MARCUS GARVEY
black nationalist leader

JOSH GIBSON
baseball great

WHOOPI GOLDBERG
entertainer

DANNY GLOVER
actor

CUBA GOODING JR.
actor

ALEX HALEY
author

PRINCE HALL
social reformer

JIMI HENDRIX
musician

MATTHEW HENSON
explorer

GREGORY HINES
performer

BILLIE HOLIDAY
singer

LENA HORNE
entertainer

WHITNEY HOUSTON
singer and actress

LANGSTON HUGHES
poet

JANET JACKSON
musician

JESSE JACKSON
civil-rights leader and politician

MICHAEL JACKSON
entertainer

SAMUEL L. JACKSON
actor

T. D. JAKES
religious leader

JACK JOHNSON
heavyweight champion

MAE JEMISON
astronaut

MAGIC JOHNSON
basketball great

SCOTT JOPLIN
composer

BARBARA JORDAN
politician

MICHAEL JORDAN
basketball great

CORETTA SCOTT KING
civil-rights leader

MARTIN LUTHER KING, JR.
civil-rights leader

LEWIS LATIMER
scientist

SPIKE LEE
filmmaker

CARL LEWIS
champion athlete

RONALD MCNAIR
astronaut

MALCOLM X
militant black leader

BOB MARLEY
musician

THURGOOD MARSHALL
Supreme Court justice

TERRY MCMILLAN
author

TONI MORRISON
author

ELIJAH MUHAMMAD
religious leader

EDDIE MURPHY
entertainer

JESSE OWENS
champion athlete

SATCHEL PAIGE
baseball great

CHARLIE PARKER
musician

ROSA PARKS
civil-rights leader

COLIN POWELL
military leader

QUEEN LATIFAH
entertainer

DELLA REESE
entertainer

PAUL ROBESON
singer and actor

JACKIE ROBINSON
baseball great

CHRIS ROCK
comedian and actor

DIANA ROSS
entertainer

AL SHARPTON
minister and activist

WILL SMITH
actor

WESLEY SNIPES
actor

CLARENCE THOMAS
Supreme Court justice

SOJOURNER TRUTH
antislavery activist

HARRIET TUBMAN
antislavery activist

NAT TURNER
slave revolt leader

TINA TURNER
entertainer

ALICE WALKER
author

MADAM C. J. WALKER
entrepreneur

BOOKER T. WASHINGTON
educator

DENZEL WASHINGTON
actor

J. C. WATTS
politician

VANESSA WILLIAMS
singer and actress

VENUS WILLIAMS
tennis star

OPRAH WINFREY
entertainer

TIGER WOODS
golf star

ON
ACHIEVEMENT

———— ❧ ————

Coretta Scott King

Before you begin this book, I hope you will ask yourself what the word *excellence* means to you. I think it's a question we should all ask, and keep asking as we grow older and change. Because the truest answer to it should never change. When you think of excellence, perhaps you think of success at work; or of becoming wealthy; or meeting the right person, getting married, and having a good family life.

Those goals are worth striving for, but there is a better way to look at excellence. As Martin Luther King Jr. said in one of his last sermons, "I want you to be first in love. I want you to be first in moral excellence. I want you to be first in generosity. If you want to be important, wonderful. If you want to be great, wonderful. But recognize that he who is greatest among you shall be your servant."

My husband knew that the true meaning of achievement is service. When I met him, in 1952, he was already ordained as a Baptist minister and was working toward a doctoral degree at Boston University. I was studying at the New England Conservatory and dreamed of accomplishments in music. We married a year later, and after I graduated the following year we moved to Montgomery, Alabama. We didn't know it then, but our notions of achievement were about to undergo a dramatic change.

You may have read or heard about what happened next. What began with the boycott of a local bus line grew into a national crusade, and by the time he was assassinated in 1968 my husband had fashioned a black movement powerful enough to shatter forever the practice of racial segregation. What you may not have read about is where he learned to resist injustice without compromising his religious beliefs.

He adopted a strategy of nonviolence from a man of a different race, who lived in a different country and even practiced a different religion. The man was Mahatma Gandhi, the great leader of India, who devoted his life to serving humanity in the spirit of love and nonviolence. It was in these principles that Martin discovered his method for social reform. More than anything else, those two principles were the key to his achievements.

These books are about African Americans who served society through the excellence of their achievements. They form part of the rich history of black men and women in America—a history of stunning accomplishments in every field of human endeavor, from literature and art to science, industry, education, diplomacy, athletics, jurisprudence, even polar exploration.

Not all of the people in this history had the same ideals, but I think you will find that all of them had something in common. Like Martin Luther King Jr., they all decided to become "drum majors" and serve humanity. In that principle—whether it was expressed in books, inventions, or song—they found a goal and a guide outside themselves that showed them a way to serve others instead of living only for themselves.

Reading the stories of these courageous men and women not only helps us discover the principles that we will use to guide our own lives; it also teaches us about our black heritage and about America itself. It is crucial for us to know the heroes and heroines of our history and to realize that the price we paid in our struggle for equality in America was dear. But we must also understand that we have gotten as far as we have partly because America's democratic system and ideals made it possible.

We are still struggling with racism and prejudice. But the great men and women in this series are a tribute to the spirit of the country in which they have flourished. And that makes their stories special and worth knowing.

1

MASTERS CHAMPION

❦

During the final round of the 1997 Masters Championship, Tiger Woods waves to the cheering gallery on the 18th fairway at Augusta National Golf Club. Moments later, Tiger would sink a five-foot par putt to become the first African American to win the prestigious tournament, breaking a slew of records in the process.

To find a wider margin of victory in a major tournament than Tiger Woods achieved in the 1997 Masters, you have to go back to '62—1862 that is. For not since Old Tom Morris won the British Open at Prestwick by 13 strokes has a golfer so dominated a major field.

Tiger's triumph is all the more remarkable because he had just turned 21, making him the youngest Masters Tournament winner in history. "He's 21 years old," said veteran pro Paul Azinger, "and he's the best player in the world." And Jack Nicklaus, who is considered the greatest golfer ever and who had held the Masters record for low score until Tiger's victory, told *Sports Illustrated*, "He's more dominant over the guys he's playing against than I ever was over the ones I played against." He also said that Woods had the talent to win as many Masters championships—10—as Nicklaus and the great Arnold Palmer won combined.

En route to his victory, Tiger tied or broke a number of long-standing Masters records that included the following (the former Masters record is in parentheses):

> Low 72 hole score: 270 (271, Jack Nicklaus, 1965, and Raymond Floyd, 1976)
>
> Widest margin of victory: 12 strokes (9 strokes, Nicklaus, 1965)

Low middle 36 holes: 131 (132, Nick Price, 1986).

Low first 54 holes: 201 (tied Raymond Floyd, 1976)

Low final 54 holes: 200 (202, Johnny Miller, 1975)

Most under par, second 9: 16 under (12 under, Arnold Palmer, 1962)

Most 3s on a winner's card: 26 (22, Horton Smith, 1936, and Tom Watson, 1977).

However impressive Tiger's win at the Masters may have been, an equally important fact about his victory was that for the first time an African American had won one of golf's major tournaments.

That it happened at the Masters Tournament was particularly fitting. In the past, Augusta National Golf Club had been typical of elite clubs in its discriminatory policies. Augusta didn't invite an African American to its showcase tournament until Lee Elder played in 1975, and didn't admit a black for membership until pressure by the Professional Golfers Association (PGA) Tour forced Augusta to do so in 1990. Tiger's win finished what Elder and other African-American pro golfers such as Charlie Sifford, Jim Dent, Calvin Peete, Jim Thorpe, and Teddy Rhodes began a generation ago. Afterward, Tiger was quick to recognize how important those pioneers were. "All night I was thinking about what they've done for me and the game of golf," he said. "Coming up 18, I said a little prayer of thanks to those guys."

Another man Tiger was quick to thank was his father, Earl. For as soon as Tiger holed his final putt, he walked over and hugged his dad. It was an unforgettable scene, both men crying softly just off the edge of the 18th green where an African American had never walked as a champion—where black men, until recently, had been welcomed only as caddies or kitchen help. But on that day, just 48 hours before the 50th anniversary of Jackie Robinson's first appearance in a major-league baseball game, Tiger Woods had shattered golf's modern-day "color barrier."

When President Clinton called Tiger Woods on Sunday night to congratulate him on his victory, he made special mention of the hug that Tiger and his father had shared. "He was proud of the way I played," Tiger said of the president's phone call. "He watched the whole tournament, but the best shot he saw all week was the shot of me hugging my dad."

In the wake of Tiger's record-setting, 18-under-par performance, veteran PGA players admitted that a new era had dawned at Augusta. "Everyone will be coming here and playing for second from now on," said Swedish golfer Jesper Parnevik. And Nicklaus, after watching Tiger hit wedges into par-5 holes that the rest of the players had to approach with long irons and woods, said that Bobby Jones should have saved the famous quote that described Nicklaus in

Nick Faldo, the 1996 Masters Champion, helps Tiger slip into the green sport jacket customarily given to the Masters champion—one of the most coveted of golf trophies.

Tiger blasts out of a sand trap on the seventh hole during the final round of his record-breaking performance. After a slow start, Woods finished with an 18-under-par score, the lowest in tournament history, and outpaced the second-place finisher by 12 strokes.

his prime—"He plays a game with which I'm not familiar"—for Tiger Woods.

But the fact is, if Tiger keeps playing at this level, everyone will soon be familiar with his game. And if he keeps winning PGA tournaments, more pros might want to side with Jeff Sluman, who jokingly declared, "I wish he would have stayed in school and got his Ph.D."

Eldrick Thon Woods was nicknamed "Tiger" in honor of a Vietnamese friend his father, Earl Woods, met while serving in the U.S. Army's elite "Green Beret" corps during the Vietnam War. Here several Green Berets instruct a Vietnamese soldier in the operation of a 57mm recoilless rifle.

2
THE EYE OF THE TIGER

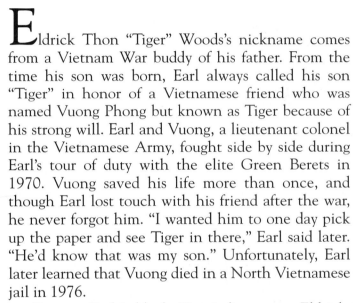

Eldrick Thon "Tiger" Woods's nickname comes from a Vietnam War buddy of his father. From the time his son was born, Earl always called his son "Tiger" in honor of a Vietnamese friend who was named Vuong Phong but known as Tiger because of his strong will. Earl and Vuong, a lieutenant colonel in the Vietnamese Army, fought side by side during Earl's tour of duty with the elite Green Berets in 1970. Vuong saved his life more than once, and though Earl lost touch with his friend after the war, he never forgot him. "I wanted him to one day pick up the paper and see Tiger in there," Earl said later. "He'd know that was my son." Unfortunately, Earl later learned that Vuong died in a North Vietnamese jail in 1976.

Because Earl is black, Tiger's first name, Eldrick, was given to recognize his African-American heritage. Thon, his middle name, is Thai, and it represents an important link with his mother's birthplace, Thailand. Tiger was raised according to traditional Thai customs and learned the basic beliefs of the Buddhist religion from his mother, Kultida. "I like Buddhism because it's a whole way of being and living," he says. "It's based on discipline and personal responsibility."

Earl Woods had never picked up a golf club until he was 43 years old and about to retire from the army.

Twenty years after Earl Woods first put a golf club in his son Tiger's hands, the elder and younger Woods share a special moment after Tiger's 1997 Masters Championship victory.

Even then it wasn't his idea. A buddy kept urging him to come out to the course and give it a try, and one day he reluctantly agreed to go along. Though Earl had been skeptical, he instantly fell in love with the game.

Earl soon became a regular on the public golf courses near his home. Knowing he was too old to ever become exceptional, he regretted that he hadn't started playing earlier. However, Earl was realistic. "I was a black kid, and golf was played at the country club—end of story," Earl said years later. "But I told myself, if I ever have a son, somehow he would get a chance to play early in life." Kultida gave birth to a son only two years after Earl had made this promise to himself, on December 30, 1975.

While most six-month-old babies are content to spill their milk or spatter their baby food, Tiger Woods had a different idea of entertainment. He loved to watch his father hit golf balls. Earl Woods practiced in the garage of the family's Cypress, California, home, hitting golf balls off an artificial grass mat into a net with a 5-iron, while his infant son sat in a high chair and studied his dad's every move. Though an average six-month-old child has an attention span of only seconds, Tiger watched intently as his father hit ball after ball. When Earl finished, he would hand a plastic putter to his son and hold him up so he could hit balls into the net also.

"It was uncanny the way he could emulate my swing," Earl said later. "It was like looking at a mirror image of myself." Earl was so amazed by his son's ability to concentrate on golf that he never moved that high chair from the garage. If you visit the Woods' home today, it's still there—a symbol of Tiger's dedication to the sport.

Once Earl was convinced of Tiger's interest in golf, he did all he could to help him hone his skills. Earl began an informal training routine when Tiger was still a baby. Knowing that balance is critical in golf, Earl played a game with Tiger. Holding out his hands, he encouraged his little son to step forward onto his palms. Earl lifted one hand and then the other. Tiger fell down giggling at first, but in a short time it became a challenge. No matter how much Earl tested him, Tiger fought to hold his balance and stay upright. When Earl made a sudden move, Tiger twisted his body. If he had to, Tiger swung his arms and swayed, but he rarely tipped over. By keeping his feet, Tiger was developing the coordination and flexibility that would allow him to play golf with exceptional power and grace.

The competitive spirit Tiger showed as a toddler became even more intense once he got a golf club in his hands. In a few short months he moved out of his high chair to hit golf balls on the front lawn, and soon he was swinging a cut-down golf club on the fairway of a nearby golf course. Tiger's ability to strike a golf ball immediately began attracting attention.

Jim Hill, a sports reporter for a Los Angeles television station, did a story on Tiger when he was still a toddler. While they were filming Tiger, Hill was so impressed that he announced, "This young man is going to be to golf what Jimmy Connors and Chris Evert were to tennis."

Since those early swings in his garage, golf has dominated Tiger's life. In fact, Tiger now says the only things that interest him beyond the sport are "sleeping and eating."

Even when he won his first event, a "pitch, putt, and drive" competition, as a 3-year-old competing against 10- and 11-year-olds, Tiger had his sights set on big goals. Chuck Brewer, the man who ran that tournament, remembers Tiger well. "What impressed me most about Tiger," says Chuck, "wasn't just that he won, but what he did after. For his prize he could have picked out a toy, a piece of golf equipment, or a trophy. He ignored the toys and took the trophy— the biggest one we had—as big as he was."

As Tiger's ability to swing a golf club improved, so did his knowledge of the game. One day when Tiger was only two years old, he looked at a grown man's golf swing and told his father what was wrong with the man's technique. "Look, Daddy," Tiger said, "that man has a reverse pivot."

The same year, he gave a putting exhibition on national television. The audience of *The Mike Dou-*

glas Show was delighted when Tiger, who was still wearing training pants, upstaged veteran comedian Bob Hope, a dedicated golfer.

When Tiger was four years old he met Rudy Duran, a pro at Heartwell Park in Long Beach, California. At first Rudy wasn't interested in looking at a preschooler's golf swing, but the minute he saw Tiger pick up a club, he changed his mind. "It was mind-boggling to see a four-and-a-half-year-old swinging like a refined touring pro," Rudy said. "It was like watching a PGA player shrunk to 50 pounds. What would Jack Nicklaus shoot if he was three foot seven? That's what Tiger shot."

With Rudy's help Tiger was soon hitting the ball even better. At five years old Tiger was a guest on the television show *That's Incredible*, and people all over America marveled at how far the little guy could rip a golf ball. He told host Fran Tarkenton, "When I get big, I'm going to beat Jack Nicklaus and Tom Watson." That same year, 1981, *Golf Digest* did its first feature article on him. By the time Tiger turned six he'd already scored two holes in one and played a golf exhibition match against Sam Snead. (He only lost by two strokes.) Amazingly, at the age of eight, he was the club champion of Heartwell Park Golf Club and won his first Optimist International Junior World title.

Though Earl gave Tiger every opportunity to play the game, Tiger practiced because he wanted to. He was hard on himself and wouldn't settle for anything but perfection. His solid swing mechanics and his amazing touch around the greens grew naturally out of his love for the game. Neither his coaches nor his father ever had to push Tiger to work on his game. When Tiger was only two years old he would call Earl at work and beg him to take him to the golf course when he got home.

The one thing Earl did insist on, though, was that Tiger work on his mental toughness. Earl pushed his son extra hard to make him ready for the pressures that come with tournament golf. When Tiger was only seven years old Earl would stand right in front of him and say, "Pretend I'm a tree," forcing his little son to loft a wedge shot high over his head.

When Tiger was still in kindergarten he asked his parents for a subliminal tape. (These are recordings that help some people learn through subtle messages and peaceful music.) Tiger loved his tapes so much that he played them over and over. Whether he was putting on the carpet, swinging in front of his

mirror, or watching videotapes of old Masters Tournaments, Tiger listened to the messages. He even printed out his favorite slogans and tacked them to the bookshelf in his bedroom. One read, "My decisions are strong! I do it all with my heart." Another read, "I focus and give it my all." A third message had a similar tone: "I will my own destiny." Though most parents would have gone crazy from the same tapes being played so often, Tiger's mom and dad encouraged him to keep it up.

Tiger's mother, Kultida, was the family disciplinarian, insisting he do his chores or finish his schoolwork before going to the golf course. Here Tiger and his mom smile proudly after his victory in the 1997 Asian Honda Classic, held in Kultida's native country, Thailand.

At age 15, after winning the 1991 U.S. Junior Amateur Championship, Tiger explained his ambition: "I want to be the Michael Jordan of golf. I want to be the best ever."

To further strengthen Tiger's powers of concentration, Earl did some unconventional things. Although many parents pamper their child athletes, Earl did the opposite. He went out of his way to be hard on Tiger and prepare him for the grueling competition he knew lay ahead.

The summer when Tiger was 12 years old Earl decided to test his son's psychological strength. For a whole month he put Tiger through a golf course torture session that neither of them will ever forget. Using mind games that he learned when he was in the Green Berets in Vietnam, Earl pushed his son to the limit. Because Earl had conditioned soldiers to endure the psychological tortures of long-term imprisonment, he knew just how far to push Tiger.

Each morning they drove to the Navy Golf Course in Long Beach, and Earl went to work on his son. Every time Tiger got ready to play a shot, Earl did something devious. Sometimes he coughed loudly or jiggled coins in his pocket just when Tiger was getting ready to take his club back. Other times he was perfectly silent until Tiger was in the middle of his backswing. Then without warning he shouted or dropped his golf bag to the ground. But he didn't stop there. He reminded Tiger not to snap hook the ball as he stood on the tee. He rolled a ball across his son's line or ripped open the Velcro fastener on his golf glove as Tiger was about to putt. And Earl cheated when he and Tiger played matches. He marked his own ball a foot closer to the hole. He kicked his ball out of the rough, but made Tiger play every bad lie he found. He wrote down a 5 for himself when he made a 6.

Then, to make matters worse, Earl proceeded to criticize each shot Tiger made. No matter how well Tiger struck the ball, Earl found fault.

"He constantly put me down," Tiger recalls. "Then when I really got mad, he'd say, 'I know you want to slam down that club, but don't you dare do it. Don't you dare!'"

Earl quit then, but only for a few minutes. As soon as his son cooled off, he started picking on him again. "He'd push me to the breaking point, then back off, push me, then back off," Tiger says. "It was wild, but you got to think that it helped. I'd get angry sometimes. But I knew it was for the betterment of me. That's what learning is all about, right?"

Looking back, his dad is confident that his unorthodox methods worked. "You could just see the boy toughen up," he says. "By the end of the month, he was pulling that stuff on me." It's clear that Tiger learned well during his dad's training sessions. Experts who watch Tiger all agree that one of his greatest strengths is his ability to concentrate, stay under control, and focus on his own game.

When Tiger entered his first tournaments, Earl talked in military terms. Tiger was always on "a mission," and he wanted his son to be nothing less than battle ready. At the end of each tournament, Earl called "debriefing" sessions to discuss what went well and what didn't. The mental training and review worked. Before Tiger entered junior high, he had won over 100 trophies in local, regional, and national events.

Tiger's mom, Kultida (Tida), is the disciplinarian in the family. While Earl is Tiger's golf buddy and coach and lets Tiger learn from his mistakes, Tida believes in swift and fair punishment. When Tiger was a child, she always reminded him to keep up his schoolwork—"No homework, no practice" was one of her favorite expressions.

Tida expects only the best conduct from her son on the golf course. Tiger lost his temper once in a junior tournament and smashed a club against his golf bag after a bad shot. When Tida saw the incident, she immediately reported Tiger to the tournament directors and requested that her son receive a two-stroke penalty.

"Mom," Tiger complained, "shut up."

Tida was furious with her son. "Who made the bad shot?" she demanded. "Whose fault was it? If you want to hit something, hit yourself in the head."

With the combined help of Earl and Tida, Tiger developed tremendous composure and concentration on the course. When Tiger was only in second grade he played in an international event, the Optimist International Junior World Tournament. Earl took him to the first tee and told him, "Son, I want you to know I love you no matter how you do. Enjoy yourself." Tiger hit a perfect drive down the middle of the fairway, and he went on to win the tournament.

When the round was over, Earl asked his son what he was thinking as he got ready to hit that first tee shot. Tiger said, "I was thinking where I wanted the ball to go, Daddy." As a second grader, Tiger was already visualizing perfect shots.

"That's when I knew how good he was going to be," Earl said later.

By the time Tiger entered junior high school, he had won more tournaments than most golfers win in a lifetime. An entire room in his home was filled from floor to ceiling with trophies. Cardboard boxes held dozens of other awards and medals that didn't fit on the shelves.

As Tiger's list of first-place finishes and record-setting performances continued to grow, he worked even harder at improving his game. When he was 15 years old, after winning the U.S. Junior Amateur Championship, he explained his ambition to the *New York Times*: "I want to be the Michael Jordan of golf. I want to be the best ever."

3

THE LOS ANGELES OPEN

O ne thing that separates Tiger from most golfers is his ability to set goals. Although many young athletes play sports to please their parents and coaches, or to impress their friends, Tiger has always been self-motivated.

One goal Tiger set when he was in junior high school was to take more control over his career. Both he and his father knew that if he wanted to be a professional golfer someday, he needed to learn how to manage his own affairs. When he was in elementary school his father scheduled his tournaments and made all the necessary reservations, but once Tiger turned 14 he started taking charge of all the details himself. He made the phone calls to reserve rooms, hire caddies, and set up practice times. "By the time he was 16, he took over full responsibility, and there was a role reversal," Earl says. "On the road, I became the child and he became the parent. He's in charge. He tells us what time to get up in the morning, when we go to the course, when we come home, where we're going out to dinner. The one thing he doesn't tell us is when to go to bed."

When the competition was over, Earl once again became the father. "As soon as the last ball was hit in the tournament, the roles would be reversed again automatically," Earl said.

Another of Tiger's goals was to play in an official

While the other sophomores at Western High School in Cypress, California, were studying English and algebra, Tiger Woods was teeing off in the 1992 Los Angeles Open, becoming the youngest person ever to play in a PGA Tour event.

PGA event as early as he possibly could. Since he lived only 40 miles from Los Angeles, the Los Angeles Open was a logical choice.

A local qualifying round is held before every professional golf tournament. This gives amateur players and nontouring pros an opportunity to become a part of the field. Because so few spots in the main tournament are open, the qualifying tournament is often tougher than the regular event. There can be as many as 200 local golfers in the field, and to make these events even more difficult for amateurs, a number of the players usually are either former PGA Tour pros who have lost their eligibility cards or members of the Asian, Nike, or Sun Coast pro golf tours, which are not as prestigious as the PGA Tour.

When Woods was 15, he decided to participate in the 1991 Los Angeles Open qualifier at Los Serranos Golf Club, even though he knew most of his competition would be seasoned professionals. Toward the beginning of his round, it looked like the Junior Amateur champion was in over his head. He hit a tree with one shot and a cart path with another. But just when he was about to shoot himself out of contention, Woods rallied for birdies on the sixth and seventh holes. After he chipped in for an eagle on the very next hole, he told Earl, who was carrying his golf bag during the day, "Don't touch me. I'm burning up."

After pars on the 12th, 13th, 14th, and 15th holes, he cracked a 344-yard drive on the par-5 16th hole, leaving only a 9-iron into the green. He hit the green and two-putted for a birdie. A par on 17 left him six strokes under par for the tournament.

As Tiger walked to his ball in the 18th fairway, Earl told him exactly what he needed to do. Earl had heard that Mac O'Grady, a PGA Tour veteran, had already posted an 8-under-par score, and another player was at 7 under. That meant Tiger needed at least a birdie to tie for second place, which would force a playoff for the final tournament spot.

Because the 18th is a par 5, Woods figured that an eagle three would tie O'Grady and win him a place in the regular tourney for certain. Tiger studied his difficult second shot. He had to hit the ball in the air 280 yards to clear a water hazard and reach the green. The ball was on a bare patch of ground that sloped downhill—a tough shot for a fairway wood.

When he swung, the dull thwack told it all. The ball splashed into the water. Tiger pulled his hat down and finished with a bogey. Though he shot a 69, a great score in anyone's book, he'd come up two strokes short.

There was no way he could hide his disappointment as he signed his card and headed to his father's Mustang. The one thing that did raise his spirits just

Riviera Country Club, a difficult course for even the best professional golfers, is the site of the Los Angeles Open.

a bit was the fact that he could still give qualifying a try again next year. He knew he would be back.

Ever since his first appearances in important tournaments, Tiger has been a favorite of fans like this one, who is wearing a "Tiger" visor.

A year later Woods was standing on the first tee of the Riviera Country Club, the golf course of Hollywood's elite. With a gallery of 3,000 people watching his every move, Tiger took a smooth backswing and then turned his body back toward the ball, snapping his wrists hard. He smashed a high drive that seemed to hang forever above the mansions that line the terraced hillside above Riviera.

"You the Kid," one man shouted from the gallery behind the tee box. The rest of the crowd applauded enthusiastically as Tiger's ball finally settled in the light rough some 280 yards from the tee.

With that swing Tiger Woods officially became the youngest golfer ever to appear in a PGA event, the 1992 Los Angeles Open. While the rest of his sophomore classmates at Western High School were studying geometry and *Julius Caesar*, 16-year-old Tiger was taking on the pros at Riviera.

Because Tiger had hit his drive out of bounds in a practice round the day before, he chose a 3-wood for his opening shot of the tournament, and it turned out to be the perfect club. Later Tiger admitted he was more nervous than he'd ever been at the beginning of a tournament: "I was so tense I had a tough time holding the club. It was like rigor mortis had set in."

Playing in front of a huge gallery was a new experience for Tiger, and it made it difficult for him to fully concentrate on his game. Though Earl had prepared his son for the potential distractions that could occur during a golf match, no amount of psychological conditioning or preplanning could ready Tiger for the enthusiasm of his fans.

Tiger was clearly moved by the thousands of people who not only came out to watch him hit his historic opening shot, but also followed him through his whole round. They cheered his good shots, and they groaned whenever he hit one poorly. One spectator even carried a "GO GET 'UM TIGER" sign to urge him on.

Responding to the crowd, Tiger hit his second shot of the 501-yard par-5 first hole onto the green. Then he two-putted for an easy birdie. Leader boards all across the course immediately registered his score: T. WOODS, -1.

"That was neat," Tiger later said of seeing his name posted on the huge scoreboard.

Less neat were his drives for most of the opening round. "He was playing army golf," Earl commented. "Left, right, left, right. But he was getting up and down like a thief. He recovered and made pars from positions that Riviera hasn't seen in a long time."

Despite the wildness of his tee shots, Tiger managed to scramble to a 1-over-par 72, which put him within range of making the cut for the weekend. A classic example of his great recoveries happened on the second hole. After a snap-hooked drive that landed near the practice range fence, Tiger bounced a weak chip off the cart path that left him 170 yards to the green. Then from behind a huge tree, he hooked an 8-iron that landed only four feet from the pin. He made his par to a volley of cheers.

Everyone who watched Tiger was impressed. "He plays the mental game like he's been out here seven or eight years," commented his caddie, Ron Matthews.

"He's remarkably mature," PGA Tour rookie Bobby Friend added.

"It was a zoo out there," said Dicky Thompson, Tiger's playing partner, commenting on the noise. "Tiger got the ball up and down from some unbelievable spots. I'd say his game is on the level of a good college player, possibly an All-American."

But the people who praised Tiger most wholeheartedly were members of his gallery. "He's the next

Nicklaus, maybe better," one fellow raved. "There walks the future of American golf," another man insisted, as Tiger holed a twisting, downhill eight-foot putt for par on the sixth.

During the second round of the tournament, Tiger shot a 3-over-par 75. That gave him a two-day total of 147, and a disappointed Woods missed the cut by six shots. Though a 75 is a score that nearly any golfer in the world would be happy to shoot at the difficult Riviera course, Tiger wanted the 69 that would have qualified him to play on Saturday and Sunday.

Tiger appreciated all the attention and support during the event. "I think these were the two best days of my life," he said afterward. "I really do. Even when I hit a bad shot people clapped."

Unfortunately there was a dark side to the tournament too. Earlier that week the tournament chairman, Mark Kuperstock, received three anonymous calls expressing outrage that the Los Angeles Open committee had granted an exemption to a minority player. One caller used racial epithets that were obviously directed toward Tiger, the only African-American golfer in the field. Who knows what additional pressure Tiger felt, being accompanied not only by his fans but also by a team of security guards who were there to protect his life?

Earl Woods was not surprised. "Let's face it," he said. "A lot of major black athletes have had threats. It just goes with the territory. I just hope this doesn't trigger ideas in other minds around the world."

Following his round, the press asked Tiger for an appraisal of his effort. "It was a learning experience," he said. "I learned I'm not that good. I've got a lot of growing to do, both physically and mentally, but I'll play these guys again—eventually."

Perhaps Tiger was being too tough on himself, because in every pro tournament, half the golfers in the field routinely miss the cut. And Tiger finished

Tiger putts from the edge of the green in the second round of the L.A. Open. Although he didn't make the cut, the 16-year-old did finish with a better score than a number of PGA Tour veterans.

ahead of 15 PGA Tour veterans, including two-time U.S. Open champ Andy North and Andrew Magee, who had won two PGA events in the previous year.

Not a bad performance for a 16-year-old who had to get back to geometry class on Monday morning.

4

THE COMEBACK KID

In his career, Tiger Woods has staged a number of comebacks that have become legendary in amateur golf circles. His first big rally, however, fell just short. It occurred in the Optimist International Junior World Tournament, which Tiger had won when he was eight and won a second time as a nine-year-old. Although he'd hoped to repeat his victory the next year, the 10-year-old found himself in a bad position—eight strokes down with only six holes to play—but he didn't give up. To the amazement of the crowd, Tiger birdied the final six holes and nearly pulled out a victory.

This closing rush gave Woods the confidence to believe that no matter how far behind he was, he always had a chance to win. From that day, his biggest rallies always seem to come in the biggest tournaments. Tiger won a record three consecutive U.S. Junior Amateur Championships, a national tournament for golfers under age 18, and in each case he came from behind to win in the final holes.

In 1991, during his first Junior Amateur, Tiger was three strokes behind going into the final 18 holes, yet he rallied to tie his opponent on the final hole. By winning the first playoff hole, the 15-year-old became the youngest player and the first African American ever to win the title. In the same tournament the very next year, he found himself in an even

Long hours spent on the practice range from the time Tiger Woods was very young led to his success as a golfer.

worse predicament—two shots back with only six holes to play—but he once again surprised his opponent with a late charge to earn the victory.

Woods's amazing string of wins continued in the 1993 U.S. Junior Amateur Championship. He was two strokes down with only two holes to go, and his opponent, Ryan Armour, could close out the match by tying his score on either of the holes. Standing on the 17th tee, Armour was confident. "I thought," said Armour, "two pars and the national title is yours."

A few minutes later Tiger knocked a 9-iron to within eight feet of the hole. Needing a birdie to win the hole, he looked long and hard at the putt. "Got to be like Nicklaus," Woods whispered to his caddie. "Got to will this in the hole." He sank the putt and pulled to within one stroke.

Taking the honor on the par-5 18th tee, Woods smashed a 300-yard drive that drifted into the light rough. Tiger's second shot found a sand trap 40 yards short of the green and left him with a near-impossible up and down to tie. Woods made it look easy, though, when he lifted a perfect shot out of the powdery sand that rolled to a stop on the green eight feet from the cup. He knocked in the putt for a birdie to win the hole and tie the match. Armour, who had assumed he only needed to par the hole to win the match, had played the hole conservatively, and after looking at Tiger's second shot from the bunker he was even more confident. "I'm thinking he'll be lucky to get it on the green, and he knocks it to within 10 feet," Armour said afterward. "How good is that?"

The tie forced a sudden-death playoff to determine the national champion. Taking advantage of his momentum, Tiger defeated the stunned Armour on the first playoff hole and won the Junior National title for a third consecutive year. In the history of the U.S. Junior Amateur Championship, which began in 1948, no other golfer has ever won more than once.

Experts who study the game marvel at Tiger's

ability to rally for so many spectacular wins, and they all have their own explanations. Greg Norman, one of the top professional golfers today, sees a fierce drive beneath Tiger's calm exterior. "He gets mad," Norman says, "which is great. He doesn't show it, but you can see it's there—the controlled fire." Jay Brunza, a sports psychologist and family friend, explains it another way. "Tiger has the gift of a champion—that

In 1993, Tiger was victorious in his bid for a third consecutive U.S. Junior Amateur Championship, charging from behind on the last two holes to tie the score, then winning in a playoff round. The 17-year-old also qualified to play in the professional Los Angeles Open again.

is, he is able to elevate to another competitive level to enhance his performance when he needs it."

Brunza was first impressed by Woods's knack for boosting his play through intense concentration when the boy was only 13. Jay worked with Tiger on a Saturday night, stressing the importance of focus for an athlete and explaining how trances and a few other mind tricks worked. The very next day, he and Woods played golf with some men at a local golf club. Halfway through the front nine, one of Brunza's friends, who was playing with Tiger and losing badly, drove his cart over to Jay and complained. "What kind of monster have you created?" he asked. "He's birdied five of the first six holes."

When Brunza tried hypnosis on Woods, it took him only a minute to put him under. In a short while he and Tiger connected so easily that Brunza could give the young golfer hypnotic suggestions over the phone. Once Jay hypnotized Tiger right in front of Earl before Dad even knew what was happening. As a joke he said, "Tiger, hold out your arm straight." When Tiger did, Brunza told Earl, "Now try to bend it." Earl pulled and pushed and hung on that arm, but his son held it rigid.

Even though Woods has been able to develop a winning mental attitude, he still feels nervous sometimes. One of those times occurred when Tiger competed at the "Big I," a national tournament sponsored by the Independent Insurance Agents of America, when he was 13. Although Tiger had been undefeated in his age group as a 12-year-old, the Big I was his first major national tournament, and he was feeling the pressure even before the event began. "I was in the shower in my hotel room, and I couldn't pick up a bar of soap," he said later. "I was choking in the shower, and I'm thinking, 'How am I going to handle this?' On the first tee I'm 100 percent nervous. . . . My eyes were looking at trees. I couldn't focus on the fairway."

Once play began, Woods hit the ball poorly for

the first six holes. On the seventh, he hit a terrible approach and was left with a long putt to save par. But that's when something clicked inside him.

"I knew I had to make that putt," he said. "I told myself, 'If you make this putt you win. This is the turning point.' And I just felt myself slow down, like the game was easy again. I knocked it in, and I busted the next drive. And I won."

Everyone gets nervous, but what separates Tiger Woods from an average player is his ability to channel and control his emotions. "Tiger's got an aura about him that you see in very few kids," says Chris Haack, the assistant director of the American Junior Golf Association. "Besides having a great swing, he shows very little emotion on the golf course. He's got the killer instinct, and he knows how to think his way around."

Today, Woods can concentrate so deeply that he has no need of hypnotic help. He has developed the ability to block out everything but the shot he has to make. The crowds and caddies and fellow competitors all fade away, especially when the match is on the line.

However, when people try to style Tiger as a robotlike golfer or as a young man who has no life beyond the golf course, they are totally wrong. Off the course, Tiger looks nothing like a killer. Tall and good-looking with a winning smile, he is perfectly at ease whether he is answering questions from reporters or entertaining an audience with an after-dinner speech.

In high school, Tiger was a typical teenager. He often had a compact disc player clipped to his belt, and he spent his Friday nights rooting for his high school football team. He liked playing touch football with his friends too, and once, he even suffered a concussion when he smacked his head on a tree. During the off season he frequently went several days in a row without picking up a golf club.

Greg Norman, one of the best golfers today, has praised Tiger's ability to block out distractions and focus on hitting perfect shots. "You can see it's there—the controlled fire," explained Norman.

Over the years he's also had to fight the same sort of bad habits and compulsions kids everywhere develop. In Tiger's case, his main problem was TV. He tried to monitor himself carefully, so he didn't waste too much time watching. He also enjoyed eating pizza, watching Michael Jordan and professional basketball games, going to football games, listening to rap music, and hanging out with friends.

"The public thinks of him as a full-time golfer," Woods's high school friend and former teammate

Byron Bell said in 1994 after Tiger won his first U.S. Amateur Championship at age 18, "but he does everything normal kids do. The only difference is he has to go out to the golf course every once in a while."

The year after winning his third-straight United States Golf Association (USGA) Junior Championship, Woods set his sights on the 1994 U.S. Men's Amateur Championship. Tiger had already competed in the U.S. Amateur three times, placing in the top 32 players twice. This time, though, he believed he could win.

He needed to use every bit of his famous concentration when he found himself three strokes down to Buddy Alexander with only five holes to go in a preliminary round. Alexander, the 41-year-old coach of the University of Florida golf team, appeared to be giving Tiger a golf lesson through the 13th hole of their match. But when the players approached the 14th tee, Earl Woods told a reporter, "It's not over yet. Tiger has one more run left in him."

Playing 1-under-par golf for the next four holes, Woods tied the match. Then the teen put the pressure on Alexander by hitting a solid drive on the 18th hole. When Alexander's tee shot found the water, Woods won the hole and the match. But as dramatic as this finish was, Tiger was saving his best for the final.

The 36-hole championship match paired him with Trip Kuehne, a senior on the Oklahoma State golf team. Woods fell four strokes behind during their morning round, and many people counted him out. Kuehne's opening score of 66 on the Tournament Player's Club in Sawgrass, Florida (the same course the pros play during their championship every March), set a pace that would have finished off a lesser player.

Knowing he needed to turn things around, Woods showered and changed clothes during the lunch break. He stayed even with Kuehne through the first eight holes, and then he mounted a charge. Tiger won the 9th and 10th holes, and then he hit a tremendous drive on the 529-yard par-5 11th hole that left him only a 4-iron to the green. His birdie left him one hole behind.

Kuehne and Woods tied the next four holes; Tiger made two incredible saves from the trees to heighten the tension. Then just when it looked as if Kuehne had control, maintaining his lead with only three holes remaining, Woods birdied the 16th to even the match. As the two players approached 17, the famous par 3 with its island green, the crowd quieted.

Tiger took extra time. After judging the wind and considering the position of the pin, he made his club selection. Though most players—PGA professionals included—are happy to just carry the water on 17 and play to the middle of the green, it was clear that Woods had his eyes on the pin. When he finally cut a high shot toward the hole 139 yards away, his ball looked as if it would find the water. Then at the last minute it skipped once and settled on the fringe only 14 feet from the hole.

Tiger's high school golf coach, Don Crosby, watched as his former pupil lined up the putt. "That is the kind of moment Tiger thrives on," he said. "He battled back to get even, and when he was on the fringe I knew he was going to make it." His coach was right. Woods dropped the birdie putt to take the lead and the crowd went wild.

A solid par on 18 made Woods the youngest U.S. Amateur champion ever. When Trip Kuehne shook Earl Woods's hand after the match was over he was gracious. "That's as good as I can play," Trip told Tiger's dad. "He deserved it."

When Earl later reflected on Tiger's win, he explained why he wasn't surprised by the comeback. In Earl's mind it was clear that all his work with Tiger had paid off. "This is the first black intuitive golfer

After winning the U.S. Junior Amateur Championship a record three consecutive times, what's left to accomplish? How about becoming the youngest player ever to win the U.S. Men's Amateur Championship, as 18-year-old Tiger did in 1994.

ever raised in the United States," he explained. "Before, black kids grew up with basketball or football or baseball from the time they could walk. The game became a part of them from the beginning. But they always learned golf too late. Not Tiger. Tiger knew how to swing a golf club before he could walk."

5

GOLF AND RACISM

Over the years Earl Woods has not only helped his son with his golf game, he has also helped Tiger sort out his identity. On race and prejudice in America, Earl says, "The boy has about two drops of black blood in him. But like I told him, in this country there are only two colors—white and nonwhite—and he ain't white."

Tiger identifies with his African-American roots, yet he is quick to point out that his background also includes relatives of Thai, Native American, Chinese, and Dutch descent. But whatever his color or race might be—whether people see him as black, Asian, or American—Tiger's desire to excel at golf has never wavered. When reporters remind him that he can be the greatest minority golfer in history, he stops them short. "I don't want to be the best black golfer on the [PGA] Tour," Tiger says. "I want to be the best golfer on the Tour."

However, Tiger knows better than anyone that being black in America, even in the '90s, can be difficult. Most people are unaware of the fact that Tiger received a death threat the night before his first appearance in the Los Angeles Open, and hardly anyone heard about the threatening phone calls that he received before 1996's Skins Game. Even fewer people know about the two women who were arrested with handguns in their possession on a golf course

Tiger Woods shows a gold medallion with an image of Buddha. Tiger, who is of African American, Thai, Chinese, Native American, and Dutch ancestry, was raised as a Buddhist by his mother, Kultida.

Following the 1997 Masters, Fuzzy Zoeller angered many people with what were perceived as racially offensive comments directed at Tiger Woods. Zoeller eventually apologized for his remarks.

in Irving, Texas, where Tiger was practicing by himself for the Byron Nelson Classic.

However, many people learned about a racial incident that occurred shortly after Woods won the Masters Tournament in April 1997. A tradition at Augusta National Golf Club lets the winner of each year's Masters choose the next year's pretournament dinner menu. After the tournament, Fuzzy Zoeller, a popular PGA Tour veteran, walked up to Tiger and urged him not to request fried chicken and collard greens at the next year's event.

The reference to a stereotypical African-American meal drew national criticism, and the national retail chain Kmart dropped its sponsorship of Zoeller. Zoeller himself withdrew from his next tournament and apologized for the insensitive remarks, although he claimed it was meant as a joke. Although Woods remained upset by the incident, he accepted the apology.

"I've had a lot worse than this," Tiger said. "Hopefully, I won't have a situation like this again, but that is highly unlikely....Over time I think we will all see that it's an incident that was good for golf. It will take some time to understand it."

Unfortunately, racism remains a fact of life for most minorities. Racial hatred played an ugly role in Tiger's life even before he was born. His mom and dad were the first nonwhite couple to move into their Cypress, California, neighborhood. Though a few of the neighbors were willing to accept the Woods family, many weren't. Earl and Kultida received some ugly stares, and shortly after they moved in, some people even pelted their house with limes. But the scariest thing of all happened one day when Tida was pregnant with Tiger. She was standing at her kitchen sink when someone shot a BB gun at the kitchen window. The pellet shattered the glass and missed her head by just a few inches.

When Tiger was only eight years old he had a nightmare that he was going to die. Though most little boys have scary dreams about dying in the clutches of a monster or falling from a high cliff, Tiger's dreams were much different. "Tiger dreamed that he'd be assassinated playing golf in the South," his father recalls. The bad dream kept recurring so vividly that it was a year and a half before Tiger quieted his mind enough to sleep through the night.

Though Earl talked with Tiger about the reality of prejudice and counseled him to ignore it as an unfortunate but unavoidable part of life, it took Tiger a long time to understand how anyone could dislike him just for the color of his skin. After many months of late-night talks, Tiger eventually accepted the fact that some people are going to hate him because he looks a little different.

Charlie Sifford, the first African American to play on the PGA Tour, hits a shot during a 1969 tournament.

"I've been able to convince him there isn't anything he can do about it," Earl reflected. "It's been an abiding principle I've taught him, that you can't worry about things over which you have no control."

Though Tiger made some good friends while he was growing up, he often felt isolated living in an all-white neighborhood. In fact, when Tiger first entered school, he was the only nonwhite kid in his kindergarten class. One day, for no reason other than the fact than he had different-colored skin, a few of his classmates tied him to a tree. Tiger was frightened and confused when they called him names and threw stones at him. Though the kids were caught and punished later, Tiger still hurts when he recalls what happened. These days he says it was no big deal, and he doesn't like to dwell on it, but he admits he will never be able to forget the incident because it marked him as a person apart. From that day forward, Tiger knew that no matter how well he did in school or how hard he tried to fit in, he would always be a little different from the rest of the class.

The first junior tournaments Tiger entered taught him another cruel lesson about prejudice. Whenever Tiger and Kultida showed up at a golf course, the other women and kids ignored them. Because it was unusual for a minority golfer to play in junior events, they stared at Tiger like he'd arrived from another planet. "I'll never forget the way those people looked at us," Tida said. "I kept telling Tiger, 'You aren't the one who has the problem. These people have the problem. These people are sick.'"

Ironically, some of the same junior golfers who used to ignore him now cluster around him after a big tournament, asking for advice and autographs, but the hurt is still there. The bitterness can't help but come out once in a while.

When Tiger talks about racism these days he chooses his words with care. No matter how much he succeeds Tiger knows there will always be a few narrow-minded people who want to convince him that he doesn't belong. "You can feel it—I call it 'The Look,'" Tiger explained. "It makes you uncomfortable, like someone is saying something without saying it. It makes me want to play even better. That's the way I am. Little things like that motivate me."

Even if Tiger wanted to downplay the issue of race, there's no way to avoid it. He can't help being a symbol of the long-overdue integration of golf. He's a reminder of the many years blacks were only allowed into country clubs as cooks and caddies.

Long after African-American athletes were playing professional basketball and baseball and football, they were still excluded from golf. Until 1962 the PGA bylaws included a whites-only clause that restricted membership to "professional golfers of Caucasian race," and Clifford Roberts, the founder of the Masters Tournament at Augusta National Golf Club, once said, "As long as I'm alive, golfers will be white and caddies will be black." Charlie Sifford, the first African American to compete on the PGA Tour, was a victim of this prejudice. Sifford was often forced to change his shoes in the parking lot, and at many clubs he had to use the caddie entrance to get onto the course. Although he should have qualified for the Masters twice, he was never permitted to play.

Lee Elder, an African American who followed Sifford on the PGA Tour, experienced similar disappointments. The saddest thing he can recall occurred during the 1970 Memphis Open. He was leading the tournament when a white spectator ducked under the gallery ropes, picked up his tee shot, and threw it out of bounds. In 1975, the 39-year-old Elder won the Monsanto Open, and with the victory he qualified to compete in the Masters Tournament at Augusta National, becoming the first African American to play in the prestigious event. Twenty-two years later, as Tiger was leaving the Augusta course after his record-shattering Masters victory, he spotted Elder in the crowd, stopped, and gave him a hug. "Thanks for making this possible," Woods whispered.

Though official policies have changed, the absence of minorities in golf today is still shocking. Statistics show that many of the nation's private clubs still do not allow African-American members. On the PGA, Ladies Professional Golf Association (LPGA), and Nike golf tours combined there is only one black golfer other than Tiger: Jim Thorpe. On the senior tour, Jim Dent is the only one approaching star quality. Of the 350 entries in the 1995 PGA Club Pro Championship, there was only one black golfer, Tom Woodward, in the entire field.

Woodward, who has followed Tiger's career with interest, knows firsthand how tough it is to advance as an African-American golfer. Even though he played three years on the PGA Tour, Woodward was unable to get a club job anywhere in Florida. Eventually he had to return to his hometown of Denver to find employment. The big money is in country club jobs, but Woodward had to settle for a position at a municipal course. "There are no blacks hired because there's no one in a position to hire them," explained Kennie Sims, an African-American golf club professional in Florida. "A pro gets hired, and he's going to bring in his own people."

At one time, blacks were only allowed in golf clubs as caddies or kitchen help. Tiger has helped raise interest in the game among young minorities.

Watson Dobbs, one of only two African-American golf pros in Southern California, has praised Tiger as being a healthy influence on the game. "Is he going to have an impact? Of course he is," said Dobbs. "There are still barriers. Tons of them. Just use your imagination. There are still country clubs, and who runs country clubs and belongs to them? So is his playing a positive influence? The answer is yes. And is he healthy for the sport? The answer is yes.

"Tiger represents a lot of good things for any minority group," Dobbs continued. "Achievement, class, intelligence. All the kids want to emulate him. He's a hero, period. He's like Michael Jordan to them. They want to swing like him. They want to play like him."

Though Tiger provided a great example for young minority golfers during his junior golf years, once his college career began, the media attention increased dramatically. After entering Stanford University on a golf scholarship, Tiger won his very first college tournament, the Tucker Invitational, with an 8-under-par total. In his third event he appeared at Shoal Creek, a golf club in Alabama that had been the site of an intense discrimination battle four years earlier, just before it was scheduled to host the 1990 PGA Championship.

When the PGA announced it would change its long-standing policy and deny tournament sponsor-

---

TIGER'S ETHNIC BACKGROUND

Just before he was to participate in the U.S. Open for the first time, in June 1995, Tiger Woods issued a statement to the media that he said would be his final comment on the subject:

My parents have taught me to always be proud of my ethnic background. Please rest assured that is, and will be, the case, past, present, and future.

The various media have portrayed me as African American, sometimes Asian. In fact, I am both. Yes, I am the product of two great cultures, one African American, the other Asian. On my father's side I am African American, on my mother's side I am Thai. Truthfully, I feel very fortunate, and equally proud, to be both African American and Asian.

The critical, and fundamental, point is that ethnic background and/or composition should not make a difference. It does not make a difference to me. The bottom line is that I am an American...and proud of it!

That is who I am and what I am. Now, with your cooperation, I hope I can just be a golfer and a human being.

ship to any club that discriminated against minorities, it looked as if many courses would lose the right to host pro tournaments. Reports showed that 17 of the 39 PGA Tour courses, including Shoal Creek, did not admit minority members. Hall Thompson, the club's founder, said his course would not be pressured into accepting black members, but under pressure from the PGA board, Shoal Creek eventually changed its policy and did allow an African-American member so it would be permitted to host the PGA Championship. Sadly, once the tournament was over, Shoal Creek continued its policy of discrimination, refusing to accept any additional minority members.

When reporters reminded Tiger of the incident before his college tournament there in 1994, he wasn't afraid to speak out. "I thought it was a sad situation," Tiger declared. "It's not supposed to be like that in the '90s. Isn't this America? Aren't we supposed to be one big melting pot?"

When Tiger shot a 67 on the final day at Shoal Creek and won by two strokes, he showed young African-American and other minority children that they can accomplish whatever they set their minds to. And afterward, when reporters asked him to comment on the racial implications of his win, he downplayed race, preferring instead to look on his accomplishment from a team perspective. "I just went out and wanted to play well," said Tiger after the round was over and he had led Stanford to the team title. "The significance to me is that our team won, and I also happened to be the individual champion. That's what we came here to do. We play to win."

Although Tiger doesn't like to get involved in racial issues that can distract him from playing his best, he does contribute to the African-American community. When he was only nine years old he saw news clips of the famine in Ethiopia and was so moved that he took $20 out of his piggy bank and

Tiger helps eight-year-old Kaleb Jordan with his swing during a golf clinic.

asked his parents if they could send it to Africa. Today, Tiger enjoys donating his time at golf clinics in poor neighborhoods, and he would love to see more young minorities take up the game. He recently established a foundation to help kids learn how to play golf, and he feels he's already seen improvement in the attitudes of children toward the game. "I think that it is already happening," he claims. "Just from the clinics I've done in the inner city, I think we're seeing an influx of minorities into golf."

The director of the Young Minority Golf Association, Jacci Woods (no relation), is a great fan of Tiger. "He's a real inspiration for kids," she said after bringing a group of young people to watch Tiger play in a Michigan tournament. "Everybody felt a kinship with him. He's become a role model for my kids. He's a pioneer." And Tiger's coach at Stanford University, Wally Goodwin, also appreciates his former star's concern for the disadvantaged. "I think he'd rather put on a clinic for kids than play in a tournament."

Even though Tiger prefers putting to preaching about racial equality, he realizes the symbolic importance he holds for minorities in America. "I know I will set the example for black golfers," he admits. "There are no ifs, ands, or buts about it. I'm doing that right now."

The first television commercial Tiger chose to appear in, a 1996 Nike spot, shows the strength of his commitment to racial equality, as he chose to speak out against prejudice. "There are still courses in the United States that I am not allowed to play because of the color of my skin...." pointed out the controversial ad.

With those words, the 20-year-old pro sent a message to America: get ready for Tiger Woods.

6

THE WORLD AMATEUR

Having won every amateur event the United States had to offer, in the summer of 1994 Tiger took his clubs overseas to compete in the World Amateur Championship. Though the American team was mainly made up of successful businessmen in their forties, 18-year-old Tiger, as the new U.S. Amateur champion, was invited to join their ranks.

The tournament was held in Versailles, France, near the site of the famous palace outside Paris. From the moment Tiger arrived, the French press swamped him with interview requests, and the reporters were impressed at his quiet confidence and maturity. Tiger proved to be so popular during the four days of play that he attracted five times as many people to his galleries as any of the local French players.

The headlines in French papers described him with nothing less than adoration. One daily paper, *Le Figaro*, compared him to the musical genius Mozart. Another, *L'Equipe*, ran a headline touting him as a terror of the golf links: TIGER LA TERREUR. One American reporter joked that Tiger's fame among the French people was nearly equal to that of their much-admired comic hero, Jerry Lewis.

When Tiger arrived at the course, Golf de La Boulie, he immediately went to work. While the rest of the American team took a tour of Paris, Tiger hit the practice range. Because he had already been to

The oldest golf course in the world, St. Andrews Royal and Ancient Course in Scotland, was the site of the 1995 British Open, where Tiger competed against some of the best golfers in the world, including Nick Faldo.

France for a junior event when he was 14, he decided to use the extra time to hone his game. Preferring to take his meals at a local McDonald's, Tiger spent his whole nine days in France focusing on the tournament. If he wasn't playing a match, he was hitting practice balls.

Tiger knew that the United States had lost five World Amateur titles in a row, and he wanted to help reverse that slide. Though the United States had dominated this event since its founding in 1958, during the last few years a different team had beaten them every single year.

As usual Tiger's work paid off. Though the two

John Daly, one of the few players on the PGA Tour who can hit the ball as far as Tiger can, overpowered the St. Andrews course to win the 1995 British Open.

elder members of the U.S. team, Allen Doyle and John Harris, did beat Tiger and Todd Dempsey, the National Collegiate Athletic Association (NCAA) champion, out of $20 during a practice round on Wednesday, once the matches started, Tiger was superb. Tiger showed his sense of humor, too, when Doyle teased him about losing the bet.

"We sort of left them there, bleeding from the nose, with the towel thrown in," Doyle joked after the practice round.

But Tiger was quick to get revenge on Doyle when a member of the British press asked whether Doyle might be twice Tiger's age. Tiger teased, "Oh, he's a lot older than that," which was the truth, because his teammate was 46.

In the opening round Tiger immediately showed his famous ability to rally. After starting with four bogeys on the front nine, he came back with three birdies and an eagle on the last four holes. The crowd roared when he hit a long 4-iron shot just 20 feet from the cup on the 507-yard 18th hole and sunk his putt to finish with a 2-under-par 70.

With Tiger's score counting in the team total after the first round (only the three best rounds of the four-man team are counted each day), the United States led Sweden by two strokes. The next day Tiger's 75 again counted in the team total, but the U.S. team fell one stroke behind Britain and Ireland. Tiger returned to the practice range and discovered a slight flaw in his footwork. "I'm going to be tough to beat now," he said.

The following day he shot a blistering 31 on the front nine and carded a 67. Along with Doyle's 69, the United States pulled into a one-shot lead. Then on the last day of competition, team captain Doyle put Tiger in the number one spot. Though it was unusual to place the youngest player on the team in the pressure-packed final threesome, Doyle was confident of his choice. "I thought that would suit Tiger," said Doyle. "He already had the crowd, and the young man is not afraid of pressure."

"I loved it," Tiger said after play was over. "My only thought was to hit solid golf shots all day long. Nothing can go wrong then."

Solid is exactly what Tiger was on Sunday. Though the U.S. team was four shots behind after nine holes, Tiger refused to get rattled. He shot a 72, which, along with Doyle's 70, led the American team to victory. After a five-year drought, the Eisenhower Trophy was once more back in American hands, and an 18-year-old had shown the best amateurs in the world why he was a force to be reckoned with in international golf.

Doyle praised Tiger's play and his attitude after the tournament was over. "As talented as he is," Doyle remarked, "Tiger's going to be better with his head than with his hands. What I really like about him is that he knows that he's a long way from where he wants to get to. In golf, the way you get better is by knowing you're not there."

The next year, Tiger participated in another internationally famous tournament, the British Open, which was held on the famous "Old Course" of St. Andrews, Scotland. Because he was the U.S. Amateur champion, Tiger was invited to join the field, and he was anxious to make the most of his appearance at St. Andrews's famed seaside links. The 1995 British Open was the 124th anniversary of the event, and through British, American, and Japanese television coverage, the world watched the tournament unfold.

St. Andrews is the oldest golf course in the world and is famous for its blind tee shots, tricky winds, and huge pot bunkers. The deep sod-faced sand traps with colorful names such as "Coffins," "Hell," and "The Principal's Nose" are enough to paralyze even the most accomplished professional golfers. To make the Old Course even trickier, it has eight double greens that sometimes require players, who are used to approach putts of 20 and 30 feet, to hit putts as long as 150 feet.

It is a course that first-time golfers rarely play well, but a look at the huge leader board below the Royal and Ancient Clubhouse after the first two rounds showed 19-year-old Tiger tied with such international superstars as Greg Norman of Australia, Tommy Nakajima of Japan, and Ian Woosnam of Wales, just six strokes behind the leaders. Former British Open champions Jack Nicklaus, Lee Trevino, and Arnold Palmer, along with 107 other golfers, were all behind Tiger.

In the third round, playing steady golf in the unpredictable winds that blow off the North Sea all day long, Tiger showed his fans patience as well as power, disappointing no one with his even par 72. During the final round on Sunday morning, winds on the Old Course reached near-gale force, and Tiger, along with a dozen others, slipped back a bit. Saturday's leaders dropped strokes early on too, and for a long time it looked as though no one wanted to win the open title. Then to everyone's surprise, long-driving John Daly, a man the British press affectionately dubbed "The Wild Thing," took charge. One of the few men in the field who could hit the ball as far Tiger, Daly overpowered the Old Course and won the open in a playoff with Constantino Rocca of Italy.

Though Tiger shot only 78 on the final day, he still beat a good number of the pros in the field. The group of scores around Tiger's included those of such superstars as Tom Kite, Ray Floyd, Palmer, and Nicklaus, and his performance proved that he was capable of contending in a major.

More importantly, the British Open taught Tiger a valuable lesson about links golf, for he learned that anyone who hopes to win in Britain needs to master the tricky winds and the fast, hard ground that is so much a part of oceanside play.

George "Buddy" Marucci was Tiger's opponent in the finals of the 1995 U.S. Men's Amateur Championship.

His experience at the British Open would help Tiger in his next tournament a month later, when he returned to the United States to defend his U.S. Amateur title. From the moment he arrived at the course in Newport, Rhode Island, Tiger was swamped with interview requests, and every reporter wanted to know the same thing: what were his chances of becoming the first person since 1983 to repeat as the U.S. Amateur Champion?

Though Tiger emphasized that each of the competitors had an excellent chance to win, sports-page headlines across America immediately declared him the favorite. That meant every player in the tournament would be trying to beat Tiger Woods. This tournament would be the ultimate test of Tiger's ability to play under pressure.

Earl Woods had seen it coming for a year. After Tiger won four major amateur events in 1994, Earl feared that 1995 might be a letdown.

"I don't know how he can ever top a year like this," Earl had commented at the conclusion of Tiger's 1994 season. "What do you do? Go back to the U.S. Amateur and get eliminated in the semifinals and you're a failure? It puts an inordinate amount of pressure on him. To get that far in the Amateur would be a great accomplishment. It would probably be more of a disappointment in the media realm than anything. But everyone in the country who understands golf would understand what an accomplishment that would be."

Once play began, Tiger won his early matches easily. Because the Newport Country Club is a seaside, links-type course similar to the Old Course at St. Andrews, Tiger's British Open experience gave him an advantage over his opponents. Playing the same sort of bump-and-run shots he'd used in Scotland, Tiger managed his game like a pro. A recent drought left the fairways so dry that Tiger was able to hit irons off the tee on all but the longest holes; his

Tiger Woods lines up a putt during the U.S. Amateur Championship. Holding a one-stroke lead in the 1995 U.S. Amateur with one hole left to play, Woods hit a perfect chip shot to seal a victory over Buddy Marucci and defend his U.S. Amateur title.

competitors were forced to hit their less-accurate drivers. Enjoying the support of the crowd and wisely ignoring the television cameras, Tiger defeated each opponent decisively.

In the semifinals, Tiger faced a 43-year-old salesman named Mark Plummer, who was an eight-time amateur champion of the state of Maine. Though Plummer had an awkward swing and was consistently 50 yards shorter off the tee than Tiger, his solid putting kept him in the match. Tiger remained patient, though, and he refused to get rattled even when Plummer made a series of scrambling pars and long birdie putts. By playing a steady game, Tiger eventually won the match.

In the final match, Tiger and his opponent, Buddy Marucci, a 43-year-old auto dealer from Berwyn, Pennsylvania, would play 36 holes, 18 in a morning round and 18 in the afternoon. Marucci, a four-time Pennsylvania state champ, put the pressure on Tiger early, taking the lead during the first 15 holes. However, although Tiger was struggling and found himself three shots down, he stayed with the conservative game that had worked so well for him through the whole tournament. His patience paid off and he won two of the next three holes to end the morning round only one shot behind.

When afternoon play began, Tiger and Buddy split hole after hole. The crowd, though clearly favoring Tiger, was impressed by the shot-making of both players. At one point Buddy and Tiger matched birdies for two consecutive holes, and throughout the day the momentum swung back and forth. Each player had several chances to take the advantage, but neither could. Tiger took a two-stroke lead when he holed a sharp-breaking downhill putt on the 34th hole of the match, but Marucci rallied to win the next hole. If he could win the final hole, he would tie the score and force a playoff with Tiger.

Knowing that a mistake would allow Marucci to

tie, Tiger lofted his second shot perfectly over the top of the flag. "I hit it straight," Tiger said, "and let the wind just ride it." As the ball spun back to within 16 inches of the cup, Tiger pumped his fist in the air.

The match was over when Buddy missed a 20-foot birdie try and conceded Tiger's tap-in. After hugging his father, Tiger was quick to credit his experience at St. Andrews, along with the practice he put into his short game, for his win. "I spent hours and hours on the range," said Tiger, whose victory was his fifth major U.S. amateur title, "and it paid dividends."

7

STANFORD UNIVERSITY

Wally Goodwin, Stanford University's golf coach, first read about Tiger Woods in *Sports Illustrated* when Tiger was just 13 years old. Although Tiger was only a seventh grader, Goodwin took the time to write him a letter, encouraging him to work hard at both school and golf and to consider attending Stanford when he finished high school.

Goodwin saved the letter that Tiger wrote in reply because it impressed him as a remarkable example of intelligence and maturity. "In my judgment," Goodwin said, "he's a better kid than a golfer."

Here's the text of Tiger's response:

Dear Coach Goodwin,

Thank you for your recent letter expressing Stanford's interest in me as a future student and golfer. At first it was hard for me to understand why a university like Stanford was interested in a 13-year-old seventh grader. But after talking with my father I have come to better understand and appreciate the honor you have given me. I further appreciate Mr. Sargent's interest in my future development by recommending me to you.

I became interested in Stanford's academics while watching the Olympics and Debbie Thomas. My goal is to obtain a quality business education. Your guidelines will be most helpful in preparing me for college life. My GPA [Grade Point Average] this year is 3.86 and I plan to keep it there or higher when I enter high school.

I am working on an exercise program to increase my strength. My April SCGA [Southern California

Tiger, on being a student at Stanford University: "Everybody's special. You have to be to get in here. So then nobody is. That's why I love the place."

69

Stanford's golf coach, Wally Goodwin, was a major reason Tiger Woods decided to attend the school.

Golf Association] handicap is 1 and I plan to play in the SCPGA [Southern California Professional Golfers Association] and maybe some AJGA [American Junior Golf Association] tournaments this summer. My goal is to win the Junior World in July for the fourth time and to become the first player to win each age bracket. Ultimately I would like to become a PGA professional. Next February I plan to go to Thailand and play in the Thai Open as an amateur.

I've heard a lot about your golf course and I would like to play it with my dad sometime in the future.

Hope to hear from you again.

Sincerely,
Tiger Woods

Before Coach Goodwin filed Tiger's letter, he circled Tiger's comment that he was in seventh grade (NCAA recruiting rules make it illegal for coaches to contact high school–age students until their senior year), and he made a note on the bottom that read "5-5/100," meaning his future prospect was five feet five inches tall and 100 pounds at the time.

Goodwin followed the rules and didn't talk with Tiger until he was a senior in high school, but by that time Tiger was already committed to Stanford. Though he did look at several other schools with great golf programs like the University of Arizona and the University of Nevada, he always knew in his heart that he wanted to play for Goodwin.

When Woods arrived at Stanford in the fall of 1994, he knew he'd have to work hard. Though he had maintained a 3.79 grade point average during his four years at Anaheim Western High School and won the Dial award, which is given to the top scholar-athlete in the nation, Tiger found college a lot tougher than high school. Because Stanford University is an elite school that accepts only the brightest candidates, its professors demand nothing less than exceptional performances. As soon as Woods registered for the fall quarter and saw his demanding schedule of classes and tournaments, he immediately decided he would have no time to watch TV. "I left it home," he said.

Once his classes started, Tiger was amazed at the intelligence of both his professors and classmates. And there were several other high-profile students attending Stanford at the same time. Fred Savage, the young star of the television show *The Wonder Years*, was a freshman just like Tiger, and two of the greatest women athletes in the country were also enrolled at the school: Dominique Dawes, an Olympic gymnast, and Kristin Folkl, a two-sport star who had recently led both the Stanford volleyball and basketball teams to NCAA championships.

With so many talented students on campus, even a superstar could lead a quieter, more normal life than at most colleges. "Everybody's special. You have to be to get in here," Woods said. "So then nobody is. That's why I love the place."

However, despite all the celebrities in attendance at Stanford, Woods did get more than his share of attention. The school's media director, Steve Raczynski, said that the college received more calls about Tiger Woods than any entering freshman in school history. During a two-week period in September of Tiger's freshman year, his staff received 75 requests from reporters for interviews or information. "We took a little poll in the office, asking what athlete has entered Stanford with more notoriety," Raczynski reported. "We had [tennis star] John McEnroe, who advanced to the Wimbledon semifinals the summer before college; [swimmer] Janet Evans, who won Olympic gold medals before coming here; [football quarterback] John Elway. None of them was in Tiger's category."

To accommodate all the requests for information, Raczynski and his staff put together a two-page pamphlet titled "Tiger Woods at a Glance," which they included in their press kit. The first section was headed "Ages 2-5."

The campus of Stanford University, considered one of the finest colleges in the country.

Though all this media attention might have been a distraction to a less mature freshman, Tiger stayed focused on his studies. Knowing that he needed to concentrate on his classes and his golf game, Tiger limited his press contact to one news conference each month.

Unlike some athletes, he refused to sign up for any cinch courses—his fall quarter schedule included math, civics, computers, and Portuguese cultural perspectives. Tiger spent his nights cramming for tests and earned a B average in his first semester.

When Tiger joined the golf team, he found that his fellow players didn't give him any special treatment. In fact, the first teammate who saw Tiger in his glasses immediately dubbed him "Urkel," after the goofy TV character on the series *Family Matters*. And as soon as they went on their first road trip, Tiger, as a lowly freshman, was assigned the job of carrying the extra luggage.

Stanford's team was a model of diversity. Though college golf tends to be dominated by upper-class whites, Wally Goodwin's top players were a mixed group. Along with Woods, they had Notah Begay, a Native American who wore an earring and dabbed his face with clay war paint before every golf meet. William Yanagisawa, another of Tiger's teammates, was a Japanese American. Yet another player, Casey Martin, was disabled by a shriveled right leg. With Steve Burdick, a member of Goodwin's 1994 national championship team, added to this mix, Stanford had a good chance to take the NCAA crown again in 1995.

Tiger competed in 13 tournaments for Stanford, winning twice, placing second three times, and finishing fourth twice. Tiger also set a Stanford record for lowest scoring average in a season (71.37 strokes per 18-hole round). He closed out his freshman year with a fifth-place finish at the NCAA Championship, which was held at Ohio State. Though the Cardinal just missed winning their predicted title, placing second at the NCAA tourney, Tiger was named First Team All-American and the Pac-10 Player of the Year.

These were great accomplishments, but earlier that spring Tiger had found himself competing in the most exciting tournament yet. Because of his 1994 U.S. Amateur win, he had been invited to play in the most exclusive golf tournament in the world, the Masters, held at Augusta National Golf Club in Augusta, Georgia. In the 61-year history of the Masters, he was only the fourth African American to participate.

Though Charlie Sifford should have qualified for the tournament in 1967, when he won the Greater Hartford Open, Masters officials ignored their usual

Tiger Woods was one of several world-class athletes who attended Stanford. Another was gymnast Dominique Dawes, a 1996 Olympic gold medalist.

entrance criteria and refused to give him an invitation. Even when Sifford won his second tourney, the 1969 Los Angeles Open, he was still excluded from play. "I did the best I could," Sifford said later. "I just came along at the wrong time. The Man [Masters chairman Clifford Roberts] didn't want blacks to play at his course." It wasn't until 1975 that Lee Elder finally broke the color barrier at Augusta. In the next 20 years only two other African Americans, Calvin Peete and Jim Thorpe, qualified to play in the Masters. In fact, the tournament had been an all-white event since Thorpe's last appearance in 1988.

An appearance at the Masters tournament was a dream fulfilled for Tiger, who had been watching videotapes of this tournament since he was a toddler, and he was determined to make the most of his opportunity. During his practice round, he showed the gallery and PGA professionals at Augusta what he could do.

Standing on the 15th tee, a short but testing par 5, he watched two-time British Open champion Nick Faldo go through his preshot routine. Faldo's drive split the fairway, carrying about 250 yards and rolling past the tee shot by the other player in the threesome, British amateur champion Lee James.

While Tiger addressed his ball, someone down the fairway glanced at the gallery and whispered, "I've never seen this many black faces outside the caddy shed here at Augusta." A few spectators nodded their heads and grinned.

As Tiger swung there was a tremendous swish of power, followed by the pure click of a perfectly struck ball. The people in the gallery stretched to watch as the shot, launched on an unbelievably high trajectory, flew 50 yards past Faldo's ball before it hit the ground. A high bounce and a short roll later, Tiger's drive finally came to rest 330 yards from the tee. He had just outdriven Faldo, one of the best golfers in the game, by 80 yards.

Though 15 is a par-5 hole, Tiger was just a 9-iron away from the green. (Even Jack Nicklaus hit a 4-iron approach shot on this hole during his famed charge to win the Masters in 1986.) Tiger took a smooth swing, and his ball flew to the green, hopped forward, then spun back to within four feet of the hole. The crowd cheered, and up and down the fairway people asked, "A nine? Surely not a 9-iron?"

When Tiger's caddie held up nine fingers to confirm his club selection, the applause and cheers got even louder. All the way to the green, well-wishers waved to Tiger and congratulated him on his fine play. When he knocked in the eagle putt, more

Two of golf's greatest players— Arnold Palmer and Jack Nicklaus—took time to speak with Tiger during a practice round for the Masters Championship. In 1995, Woods became the fourth African American to play in the tournament. After winning a trophy as the low amateur in the field, Tiger called the event "the most wonderful week of my life."

applause followed. Several people who recognized Earl Woods in the gallery patted him on the back and told him he should be proud of his fine son.

Afterward, when a reporter asked Tiger Woods his goal for the week, the answer was simple and totally serious: "To win."

Earlier that week, when a writer from *Newsweek* had asked him the same question, he'd been more specific. "Doing well is winning," Tiger said. "To walk where Jones and Nicklaus walked, that will be daunting. But I'm not afraid of the Masters. I've never been afraid of anything. I'm going down there to win."

Once the tournament began, Tiger's play was steady for the first two days. He made the tournament cut by shooting par 72s in the first two rounds on Thursday and Friday, placing him in the middle of the pack. Though a 77 on the third day put him out of contention, Tiger recorded another even-par 72 on Sunday. His four-day total was the lowest score by an amateur, so he won a sterling silver cup. All in all, it was a pretty good showing for a 19-year-old first-time Masters participant, but Woods knew he could have scored a lot lower. "It's been a great week, but I'm about 15 shots behind where I wanted to be," he said. "I was hitting the ball great, but my iron play was inconsistent."

As he was getting ready to leave the "Crow's Nest," the rooms above the clubhouse where amateurs stay, Woods penned a thank-you note to the officers, tournament staff, and the members of the Augusta National Golf Club:

> Please accept my sincere thanks for providing me the opportunity to experience the most wonderful week of my life. It was fantasy land and Disney World all wrapped into one.
>
> I was treated like a gentleman throughout my stay and I trust I responded in kind. The "Crow's Nest" will always remain in my heart and your magnificent golf course will provide a continuing challenge throughout my amateur and professional career.

I've accomplished much here and learned even more. Your tournament will always hold a special place in my heart as the place where I made my first PGA cut, and at a major yet! It is here that I left my youth and became a man. For that I will be eternally in your debt.

With warmest regards and deepest appreciation, I remain,

Sincerely,
Tiger Woods

Such a gracious letter not only provided a perfect conclusion to the week, but it also hinted at great things that were soon to come. Two short years later, Tiger received his first green jacket from Faldo, the 1996 winner. And considering the way Woods dominated the field, the tournament committee had better make sure they have a large supply of 42 longs in stock. For as soon as he compiled his record 18-under-par total of 270 and won by a whopping 12 strokes—the highest winning margin in a major tournament since the 1862 British Open—every player in the tournament declared Tiger Woods the man to beat from that day forward.

8

TURNING PRO

W inning a championship is quite an accomplishment. Repeating as champion is a rare feat in sports. "Three-peating"—winning a championship three times in a row—is so difficult that it hardly ever occurs. No golfer had ever won three consecutive U.S. Amateur titles in the 102-year history of the event.

During the summer of 1996 Tiger Woods rewrote the golf history books. Not only did he win the NCAA Individual Championship and a record-setting third consecutive Men's Amateur Championship, but he also won two professional golf tournaments and banked an incredible $734,000 in half a season on the PGA Tour.

In his sophomore year of college, after winning his second consecutive U.S. Amateur championship, Woods remained solid for Stanford. Although the Cardinal had not been able to win the NCAA title in 1995, Woods put on a show in the NCAA Championship the next year that eclipsed his fifth-place freshman finish.

The Honors Course in Ooltewah, Tennessee, was the site of the 1996 NCAA Championship, and the joke of the week was that "Ooltewah" was a Cherokee Indian word meaning "double bogey." For every player in the field but Tiger, the joke got old fast. Ooltewah was as difficult as any PGA course. "This is

Woods's face shows total concentration as he lines up a putt.

just a great test of golf," said one coach. "It tests every aspect of your game and your courage." The course was so long—7,039 yards—and so tough that no one except Tiger could break par.

Tiger's opening rounds of 69, 67, and 69 put him so far ahead of the elite field that he was uncatchable. Even with an 80 on the final day, Tiger recorded an 3-under-par total that was four strokes better than the second-place finisher, Rory Sabbatini of Arizona. Sabbatini's team, which won the NCAA Championship, carded a humbling total score that was 34 strokes over par.

The difficulty of Ooltewah made Tiger's perfor-

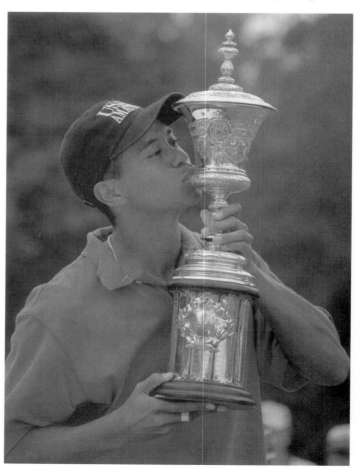

After blowing away the field on the difficult Ooltewah golf course to win the NCAA title, Tiger became the first player ever to win three consecutive U.S. Men's Amateur championships. With nothing left to prove as an amateur, on August 27, 1996, Woods announced he would turn pro.

mance even more impressive to both the competitors and coaches. "I don't believe there's any doubt he is the best player here, and the best player should win," said Bud Still, an All-American golfer from Arkansas.

The day after winning his NCAA individual championship, Tiger was invited to Muirfield Village and was presented the Jack Nicklaus College Player of the Year award by the College Golf Foundation. Tiger also had a chance to visit with the man he's modeled his career after. "Jack and I talked this year at the Masters when we played our practice round, and he helped me out a lot," Woods said. "He said some very, very nice things and some things that, you know, I took to heart."

After winning the NCAA Division I Tournament, Woods flew to England in July to compete in the British Open. Appearing for the second consecutive year at the Open, Tiger recorded the lowest total of any amateur in the championship. In one round he shot an incredible 66, which proved that the 20-year-old could hold his own with the best golfers in the world.

The next stop was the United States Men's Amateur Championship in Cornelius, Oregon. Though nearly all modern tournaments follow a stroke-play format, the Amateur is a weeklong series of grueling, head-to-head matches. Tiger's matches were made even tougher by the fact that he was the defending two-time champion, and tens of thousands of fans and reporters had traveled to Pumpkin Ridge Golf Club to study his every move.

Early in the week his wins came easily, and for a while it looked as if Woods was going to retain his crown without being tested. Then came his 36-hole final against Steve Scott. Scott, who had been hot all week, took a five-stroke lead over Tiger going into the final 18 holes.

During the lunch break, Tiger worked with his swing coach, Butch Harmon, and got back in sync.

Tiger Woods shows his excitement after a hole in one during the final round of his first golf tournament as a professional, the Greater Milwaukee Open. His enthusiasm, booming drives, and willingness to "go for it" on the golf course have made him very popular among golf fans.

He birdied four holes on the front nine and pulled to within a single shot. However, Scott fought back by holing a pitch shot to win the 10th. Then Scott countered Woods's eagle on 11 with a birdie on 14. The seesaw battle continued through the 16th, which Tiger birdied to pull to back within one shot.

A poor approach shot on 17 left Woods 30 feet from the hole. Facing the real possibility of a three-putt, Tiger stunned Scott by rolling in his first putt for a birdie to tie the match. "He knows how to deliver the death blow," said Scott of that match-tying putt. "He is not afraid to attack, and he knows when to do it. He's unbelievable."

Woods and Scott tied the 18th hole to force a sudden-death playoff. Two holes into the playoff, Tiger nailed a 6-iron that gave him a tap-in birdie and the victory. His third consecutive Men's Amateur title—even the legendary Bobby Jones could only win two in a row—capped off an amateur career that included a match record of 36-3, a higher percentage than Jones's career total of 43-8. Tiger's three consecutive U.S. Amateur Championships along with his three Junior Amateur crowns made him, at age 20, arguably the greatest amateur golfer in history. Factor in his World Optimist titles and his Junior World Opens, and the case for Tiger becomes even stronger.

As rewarding as Tiger's Amateur victory was, it also led to a personal dilemma. Although Woods had always planned to finish college before he turned professional, his NCAA and U.S. Amateur wins left him with nothing more to accomplish in the world of amateur golf. After talking with his parents, his golf instructor, and his coach at Stanford University, Tiger decided to turn professional.

Arnold Palmer, for one, agreed with Tiger's choice, saying, "As far as his amateur career is concerned, anything from here on would be anticlimactic."

Lee Trevino not only agreed with Tiger's decision, but he also urged PGA commissioner Tim Finchem to allow Tiger to join the tour without going to the PGA qualifying school. "I'd go to the board," Trevino said, "and say, 'We have an exception here.' People always say, 'Where do you draw the line?' You draw it at three U.S. Amateurs."

Despite Trevino's advice, Finchem decided to make no exceptions. If Tiger wanted to avoid the qualifying school, that left him with only one option to qualify for the 1997 PGA Tour—he needed to win enough money in the remaining events of 1996 to finish among the top 125 players. That gave Tiger only eight weeks to win approximately $150,000.

Most experts said Woods had little or no chance to make the exempt list. After all, there were over 150 professional golfers who hadn't won that much money since the 1996 PGA Tour season began in January. It was ridiculous to suggest that a tour rookie could accomplish in eight weeks what many longtime professionals hadn't been able to do in eight months.

However, Woods didn't let the skeptics bother him. And to boost his confidence, one voice, as

Tiger signs an autograph for a fan before a PGA tournament.

always, remained totally optimistic. His dad predicted that, given seven chances, not only would Tiger qualify for next year's tour, but he would also win one tournament.

Whether people agreed with Earl or not, one thing they couldn't argue with was that Tiger cashed in the day he turned pro. After an all-night negotiating session, Tiger signed endorsement contracts with both Nike and Titleist that made him one of the wealthiest athletes in the world. Estimates of the five-year deals ranged from $40 million to $60 million. Tiger's name, which had often made international headlines on sports pages, was now being mentioned just as often in the financial sections of newspapers. In the eyes of a world that equates money with success, Tiger was now an official superstar.

When Tiger arrived at his first pro tourney, the Greater Milwaukee Open (GMO), he was still tired from his tough week at the Amateur. The distractions of all the media and fan attention were a strain too. Every person in America suddenly wanted to see Tiger play.

GMO executive director Tom Strong said of the first round, "I would estimate the crowd at 20,000. It's kind of hard to tell, though, because everybody was following one guy [Tiger]." Though he opened with a solid 67, Tiger was still tired from his grueling week at the Amateur, and his play was inconsistent. When he finished in 60th place, critics pointed to the mere $2,544 Tiger had won and said that it would take him a year or two to win on the PGA Tour.

However, the very next week Tiger finished 11th in the Canadian Open, an international event that featured some of the world's best players. His $40,044 paycheck moved him to 204th place on the PGA money list.

During the next two weeks, ties for fifth in the Quad Cities and third in the B.C. Open gave Tiger $140,194 in total winnings and an almost certain

In only his fifth event, the 1996 Las Vegas Invitational, Tiger Woods became a winner on the PGA Tour.

place on the 1997 PGA Tour. Knowing he'd accomplished his first goal as a professional, Tiger decided to take a week off and skip the Buick Open. His critics were more vocal than ever, but Tiger knew that he desperately needed rest.

Tiger's stunning triumph in the Las Vegas Invitational the next week silenced the naysayers for good. After shooting rounds of 70-63-68-67-64, he beat tour veteran Davis Love III in a playoff. "He's obviously the next great player," said Love, "and we're all going to have to work to beat him." His $297,000 check vaulted him to 40th on the money list.

The drama heightened when his third-place finish at the Texas Open gave him more than half a million dollars in total winnings and moved him up to 34th place.

Then with the eyes of the sports world watching, Tiger played his best golf yet as a professional in the Walt Disney Classic. His scores of 69-63-69 on the first three days tied Tiger with Payne Stewart and set up Sunday's dramatic pairing.

Tiger is always at his best when he's playing head-to-head, and the final round at Disney was no exception. He matched Stewart's birdies all day long. Then on the pivotal 12th hole, after Stewart had hit his approach close, Tiger answered by nearly holing a 9-iron. Tiger's tap-in birdie gave him a one-stroke lead that he held to the finish. He carded a 66 in the final round to win his second tournament in only three weeks.

Stewart was generous in defeat saying, "All the accolades need to go to Tiger. Everything I've heard about how mature he handles himself, how he handles his game, it was evident today."

The $216,000 that Tiger won brought his season-ending total to $734,794, good for 23rd place on the PGA money list and a spot in the tour championship, where he placed 24th and won an additional $55,800. Not bad for a rookie of only eight events.

His record for 1996 showed astonishing improvement:

Event	Place	Winnings	Total	Tour Ranking
Milwaukee Open	T60	$2,544	$2,544	T346
Canadian Open	11	$37,500	$40,044	204
Quad Cities	T5	$42,150	$82,195	166
B.C. Open	T3	$58,000	$140,194	128
Las Vegas Invitational	1	$297,000	$437,194	40
Texas Open	3	$81,600	$518,794	34
Disney Classic	1	$216,000	$734,794	23
Tour Championship	T24	$55,800	$790,594	24

Woods's earnings, $790,594, represented the second-highest total ever for a first-year player. In 1995, David Duval set the PGA Tour's rookie record for earnings by winning $881,436—but it took him 26 events.

During the fall of 1996 virtually every magazine and newspaper in America ran lead stories featuring Tiger. He appeared on the cover of *Time* and *Newsweek*. Both the *New York Times* and the *Los Angeles Times* gave him front-page attention.

In November 1996 *Golf Digest* featured a Tiger Woods cover that simply asked, "IS THIS KID SUPER-MAN?" *Sports Illustrated* then nominated him as its Sportsman of the Year. Their lead article, titled "The

Chosen One," opened with a bold statement: "Tiger Woods was raised to believe that his destiny is not only to be the greatest golfer ever, but also to change the world."

Tiger started 1997, his first full season on the tour, quickly, winning the first tournament he participated in, the Mercedes Championship, held in January at Carlsbad, California. Tiger defeated Tom Lehman in a playoff after both finished the three-round event 14 strokes under par. He then finished 18th in the Phoenix Open and second in the Pebble Beach Pro-Am before winning the Asian Honda Classic by 10 strokes. This victory was particularly sweet for Tiger because the tournament was held in his mother's homeland, Thailand.

Woods followed with strong performances in the Australian Masters (tied for 8th), the Nissan Open (20th), the Bay Hill Invitational (tied for 9th), and the Players Championship (31st) before his spectacular, record-breaking Masters victory on April 13, 1997. He followed that win with a victory in the GTE Byron Nelson Classic in May, shooting back-to-back 64s in the first two rounds on the way to a 17-under-par score, then he placed fourth in the Mastercard Colonial at the end of the month.

By the end of the season, Woods had won four PGA tournaments in addition to the nontour Honda Classic and was the leading moneywinner on the PGA Tour, with over $2 million in winnings, eclipsing the previous record for earnings in a year.

More important, however, was his impact on the sport. Tiger attracted many nongolfers and new fans to the sport, and experts conservatively estimated his value to golf as $650 million in greater tournament attendance, merchandise sales, and lucrative new television contracts during his first year. The final rounds of 1997's four major championships—the Masters, British Open, U.S. Open, and PGA Championship—were watched in 30.3 million homes, a 56 percent increase over 1996, when 19.4 million watched. CBS Sports's golf ratings increased 24 percent in 1997, and ticket sales at tournaments in which Woods participated increased by a significant amount.

"Tiger has introduced golf to a new audience," said Dede Patterson, director of the Buick Classic tournament. Because Tiger was playing, advance ticket sales for the event were up 35 percent from the previous year. "Just the thought of Tiger boosts ticket sales," Patterson said.

With Woods's success, particularly his landmark Masters win, "Tiger mania" hit America hard, and Woods became an inspiration for young people everywhere. If Tiger Woods could be a superstar, then any kid who worked hard enough—regardless of the color of his skin or the size of his bank account—could do it too.

I plan to do more

9

WHAT THE FUTURE HOLDS

T here are two questions commonly asked about Tiger Woods: Just how good is he? and How much better can he get?

The first question is easy. He is the most successful and most publicized player of his age to ever take up the game. The only other young player who has received anything like Tiger's acclaim was the great Bobby Jones, who advanced to the quarterfinals of the U.S. Amateur back in 1916 when he was only 14 years old. Comparisons with Jones are difficult, however, because he played in a time when golf clubs had heavy hickory wood shafts, unlike the lightweight graphite shafts used today. Also, Jones remained an amateur his entire career and retired from competition before his 30th birthday.

Tiger's amateur career certainly matches up well against Jones. Although Jones won more matches in his career (43), Tiger has a higher winning percentage (.923) in amateur match play than Jones's career mark (.843). And while Jones won more U.S. Amateur titles (five) than any other player, and won back-to-back titles in 1924-25 and 1927-28, he was never able to win the U.S. Amateur crown three consecutive years, as Tiger did from 1994-96.

Modern golfers are measured against a different standard, the great Jack Nicklaus. Based on his 20 major championships, Nicklaus is recognized as the

Since turning pro, Tiger has become one of the highest-paid athletes in the world because of his endorsement deals with companies such as Nike, Titleist, and American Express. As the advertisement says, however, he has done more—helping to attract new fans and minority players to golf while becoming one of the best players on the pro tour.

So far, Tiger's career compares favorably to that of Jack Nicklaus (right), who is considered the greatest golfer of all time.

best player of our time, and most experts agree that he is the best to ever take up the game.

In a comparison of their golf career and accomplishments, Tiger fares pretty well against the Golden Bear so far.

	Jack Nicklaus	Tiger Woods
Introduced to golf	10 yrs.	9 mos.
Broke 50 (9 holes)	10 yrs.	3 yrs.
Hole in one	16 yrs.	6 yrs.
Broke 80 (18 holes)	12 yrs.	8 yrs.
Broke 70	13 yrs.	12 yrs.
U.S. Amateur Champion	19 yrs.	18 yrs.
First Masters appearance	20 yrs.	19 yrs.
First professional win	22 yrs.	20 yrs.
First major tournament win	22 yrs.	21 yrs.

When the comparison is extended to include their earliest professional tournaments, Tiger still comes out on top. Though Tiger won in only his fifth tourney, Nicklaus's best was a tie for fifteenth place in his first five weeks on tour.

Nicklaus, 1962		Woods, 1996	
Los Angeles Open	T50–$33	Milwaukee Open	T60–$2,544
San Diego Open	T15–$550	Canadian Open	11–$37,500
Bing Crosby Pro-Am	T23–$450	Quad Cities	T5–$42,150
Lucky International	T47–$63	B.C. Open	T3–$58,000
Palm Springs Classic	T32–$164	Las Vegas Invitational	1–$297,000
Total winnings	$1,260	*Total winnings*	$437,194

Question number two—How good can Tiger get?—is not as simple to answer. Child prodigies tend to be caught by their peers as they grow older, because children who start fast often burn out before they reach their full potential. Teenage tennis stars Jennifer Capriati and Tracy Austin are classic examples of players who enjoyed athletic success at a very

young age but ran into difficulty along the way. Too much too soon is not always good.

There is also evidence that Tiger is becoming tired of all the media attention. It is increasingly difficult for him to find privacy. Even when he was still in college it was so bad that the only person on campus who had Tiger's telephone number was Coach Goodwin. Now that he's turned professional, the attention has multiplied a hundredfold.

In order to give himself time to practice, Tiger is often forced to say no to reporters. The golf course, in fact, has become a refuge for him—a rare, quiet place where he can have a few hours to himself. When Tiger does grant time to writers, he often looks bored from having to answer the same questions. Though he remains polite, his face hints that it is not always easy for him to be patient.

Will Tiger crash and burn like so many other young stars? There is much in Tiger's background and his personality that indicates he won't. The people who know him best insist that he has what it takes. Greg Norman, in fact, claims that Tiger is the rare sort of talent who only appears on the golf scene every 20 or 25 years.

"This is not a fleeting ability," says his former coach, Rudy Duran. "Tiger knows how to golf. He's not going to lose that."

Nicklaus himself agrees that Tiger has all the shots. "This kid," he says, "is the most fundamentally sound golfer I have ever seen."

Byron Nelson, a retired PGA Tour star who has seen Tiger play several times, is another fan. Nelson studied Tiger during a practice round for the American Junior Golf Association Championship early in his career and couldn't find a single flaw. "I've watched him about six or eight holes," said Nelson, "and I don't see any weaknesses." From the man who won a record 13 straight PGA events in a single year, this is high praise indeed.

But as impressive as Tiger's physical ability is, his mental aptitude is even greater. At the championship level the mental aspect of the game is critically important. All the great players—Jones, Nicklaus, Hogan—have been great thinkers. Every PGA golfer has the physical talent to win, yet only a handful have the mind-set that makes it possible.

There isn't a player alive who controls his mind better than Tiger. He has developed the ability to block out negative thoughts to the point where he doesn't allow himself to even consider the possibility of hitting a poor shot. He focuses so clearly that he's "in the zone"—that elusive state of mind where training and instinct take over—more often than any young golfer in the world. "My body knows how to play golf," he explains. "I've trained it to do that. It's just a matter of keeping my conscious mind out of it."

As good as Tiger is, he is the first to admit he needs to get better. When he was asked what he needed to work on before the start of the 1997 golf season, he said, "Everything. Even if you're the best in the world at one aspect of the game, you can always improve on it."

Another major factor that should help Tiger realize continued success is his parents. Earl and Kultida have always guided and encouraged him, although the motivation and the drive have all been Tiger's. Ever since he watched his father hit balls in the garage, Tiger has been consumed by the game. Another thing in Tiger's favor is the fact that he has always loved to practice. He works on his game, not because someone wants him to, but because it gives him joy.

It was the same way with hockey great Wayne Gretzky. Whenever parents bring youth hockey players to Gretzky and say, "Wayne, will you tell him he's got to practice," he always says the same thing: "Nobody ever told me to practice."

From the time Tiger began begging his father to take him to the golf course as a two-year-old, the problem wasn't getting Tiger to practice but convincing him to come home and rest. As a four-year-old Tiger would often spend all day at the course on Saturdays. The trophies, awards, and money he has won to this point remain incidental to Tiger's love of the game.

Earl and Kultida Woods both appreciate Tiger's rare gifts. They realize that they've been privileged to witness the growth of the greatest golf talent of our time. "I know I was personally selected by God," Earl believes, "to nurture this young man…and bring him to the point where he can make his contribution to humanity."

Both parents support Tiger wholeheartedly in his

attempt to become a dominant force in professional golf, yet they remain realistic. They both know that the sports world is a fickle place where an injury can end a career in the blink of an eye. They hope for the best, but they know the ultimate destiny of their child is out of their hands.

Tiger respects and admires his parents too. "Earl is the coolest guy I know," Tiger says. "He doesn't live through me, which is what some parents do. He might watch me play, but I don't think about him on the golf course. I just think about me."

And as much as Earl has relished Tiger's triumphs, he never pushes him to take on anything he isn't ready for. Kultida also hates to see undue pressure put on her son. "He does not have to be Jack Nicklaus," she says.

Despite Tida's worries, Tiger has thrived under pressure like no one else in the history of the game. Though the media picked Tiger as a favorite in the '95 and '96 Amateurs and millions of television viewers followed every match he played, he still repeated as champion. And when it comes down to the final holes of any tournament, Tiger is often the one who's making the charge. Though he should be in awe of the older, more experienced professionals he plays with, Tiger consistently raises his game to match the level of his competition.

Beginning with his grade school and junior high exhibitions against Nicklaus, Norman, and Snead, Tiger never gave a hint of being intimidated. When he was still in high school, Tiger carded a 69 in the Insurance Youth Classic and beat 18 of the 21 professional golfers who were in the field.

When Tiger played a practice round with Palmer, Nicklaus, and Norman at the 1996 Masters, the three veterans were stunned by Tiger's power. Norman, one of the longer drivers on PGA Tour, confessed, "He was blowing it 50 and 60 yards past me. It makes you feel inferior."

Tiger's tireless work ethic has paid off. The hours he's logged on the course and at the driving range have resulted in numerous championship and tournament wins.

Another factor that weighs in Tiger's favor is his work ethic. At Stanford, if you wanted to find Tiger after classes were over, the first place to check was the practice range. It didn't matter if the wind and rain were blowing in off the ocean, chances were good that he'd be out there.

These days Tiger still spends many hours on the range, drilling ball after ball toward imaginary targets. He relishes the same games he played as a little boy, and every fluid swing is made under simulated, major-championship pressure.

Lining up one shot, he pretends he needs to drive it long and straight to keep the pressure on his nearest pursuer in a down-to-the-wire battle for the U.S.

Open title. A moment later he's forced to hit a string of perfect shots to rally from behind and win the Masters. To no one's surprise, Tiger comes out on top every time, too, because no one is tougher than Tiger when it comes to mind games. Even if he hits one in the woods or finds a bunker on his imaginary course, he always believes he will recover.

But what would happen if Tiger got sick of hitting those thousands of golf balls one day and decided to give up the game altogether? According to Jay Brunza, a longtime friend of the Woods family, Earl and Tida could handle it. Brunza says, "I think they'd say, 'Great, Tiger. We're behind you 100 percent,' and kiss him on the forehead."

Earl Woods agrees when he's asked to reflect on what he'd do if Tiger's golf career doesn't work out. "If he should fail at this," Earl says, speaking with the sureness of a man who understands life, "we'll be his parachute. He'll land softly."

Considering all of Tiger Woods's talent, however, chances are good that's one chute he'll never have to open.

CHRONOLOGY

——— ❧ ———

1975   Born Eldrick Thon Woods on December 30 in Cypress, California

1978   Makes first television appearance; wins first golf competition, a pitch, putt, and drive contest in Cypress

1979   Shoots score of 48 for nine holes on U.S. Navy Golf Course

1981   Records first hole in one

1983   Wins Optimist International Junior World Championship

1984   Repeats as Optimist International Junior World champion

1991   Becomes, at age 15, the youngest player and first African American to win the United States Golf Association's Junior Amateur Championship

1992   Repeats as Junior Amateur champion, the first player to win back-to-back Junior Amateur titles; becomes the youngest player (at 16 years, two months) to play in a PGA tournament, the Los Angeles Open

1993   Wins third U.S.G.A. Junior Amateur title; places in the top 32 in the U.S. Amateur Championship

1994   Becomes the youngest player ever to win the U.S. Amateur Championship with comeback victory in final holes over Trip Kehune; helps U.S. team win World Amateur cup during international tournament in France

1995   Repeats as U.S. Amateur Champion; becomes only the fourth African American to participate in the Masters Tournament at Augusta National Golf Club

1996   Blows away the field to easily win the NCAA championship as a sophomore at Stanford University; wins an unprecedented third consective U.S. Amateur championship; plays on America's Walker Cup team in international competition; decides to become a professional and signs endorsement deals with Nike and Titleist worth over $60 million; wins his first professional tournament; the Las Vegas Invitational; is named "Athlete of the Year" by *Sports Illustrated*

1997   Shoots 12-under-par score en route to runaway victory at the Masters Championship in April, becoming the first African American and the youngest player ever to win the prestigious event; shatters PGA record for earnings in a year; participates in international competition on the U.S. Davis Cup team; ranked number two golfer in the world for the year, finishing behind Greg Norman

1998   Wins BellSouth Classic, Johnnie Walker Classic, and MasterCard PGA Grand Slam of Golf; becomes youngest-ever number one golfer for the year in the world rankings

1999   Wins Buick Invitational by matching tournament record of 22-under par at Torrey Pines

2000   Sets or ties 27 PGA Tour records and places him among the game's greats; wins three consecutive major championships—the US Open, British Open, and PGA Championship—a career Grand Slam, and nine PGA Tour victories

2001   Captures five PGA Tour events boosting his total to 29 wins in 123 career starts; wins Masters Tournament, becoming the first player to simultaneously hold all four professional major titles; wins PGA Tour and PGA Player of the Year honors for the third consecutive year and the fourth time in five seasons; increases record as No. 1 player in the Official World Golf Ranking to 116 straight weeks

AN OVERVIEW OF GOLF

———————— ❧ ————————

Golf is one of the oldest, and most popular, sports in the world. Scotland is credited as the birthplace of golf over 500 years ago. In the mid-15th century, the game was so popular in Scotland that King James II outlawed it for a time so the citizens would devote more time to practicing archery, a sport more important to the national defense.

Today, more than 20 million people, both men and women, throughout the world play golf. Nearly half of that number are Americans, and the United States has over 20,000 golf courses. There are golf courses located in countries below sea level, at elevations of more than 14,000 feet, in deserts and forests, within the Arctic Circle, and in tropical jungles.

Two organizations set the rules of golf: the Royal and Ancient Golf Club of St. Andrews in Scotland, which was established in 1754, and the United States Golf Association (USGA), which was formed in 1894. Professional golfers are governed by the Professional Golfers Association (PGA).

The object of the game is to play a ball from a starting place, or *teeing ground*, into a 4-1/2-inch diameter cup, usually between 135 and 550 yards away, in the lowest possible number of strokes. A round of golf is 18 holes, and each hole on the course has a teeing ground; a *green*, which is a closely mowed area of grass that contains the cup; a *fairway* of low-cut grass leading from the teeing ground to the green; a area of higher grass bordering the fairway called the *rough*; and, possibly, various hazards, such as a pond that the ball must be hit over, or shallow pits filled with soft sand called *bunkers*.

Equipment

To move the ball from the teeing ground to the green, a golfer uses various golf clubs. Each golfer is allowed to use 14 clubs during his round. All golf clubs have a grip made of rubber or leather, a shaft made of steel or graphite, and a club head. The player swings the club, striking the ball on the face of the club head to move it toward the hole. There are two types of clubs: woods and irons. The woods—which despite their name are often made with aluminum, titanium, or composite clubheads instead of the wooden heads favored by early golfers—are used for long shots, especially from the tee, while the irons are used for shorter shots from the fairway or the rough.

The irons are numbered one through nine, with the number corresponding to the angle of the face of the club—the higher the number, the greater the angle. Clubs with greater angle, or loft, will lift short shots high in the air. For example, a player who is 90 yards away from the green might use a 9-iron to pitch a high shot near the cup, because the angle on that club is usually about 50 degrees. The same player would hit a 2-iron when playing a shot from 180 yards away. Although the ball will not go as high in the air, the 20 degree loft of the 2-iron allows the golfer to hit for longer distance.

Like the irons, woods are also distinguished by the degree of club face angle, with the driver, or number one wood, usually used from the tee. The driver's loft is usually about 10 degrees. Two, three, and four woods, with more loft, are often used for long shots on the fairway.

There are some clubs used for special purposes. Wedges are used for short shots, or pitching, around the green. A sand wedge is a club with a heavy head that players use to escape from a sand bunker. A putter is arguably the golfer's most important club. The putter, which has a flat face, is used on the green to move the ball into the hole.

A golf ball weighs about 1.6 ounces and is about 1.7 inches in diameter. Balls are made of rubber wound around a solid or liquid core and covered in hard, dimpled plastic. The dimples help the ball to fly farther and straighter than a smooth ball would.

Basic Rules

Once a player tees up a ball at the start of a hole, every stroke he takes until the ball is in the cup is counted toward his score. Each hole has a *par* score, which is the number of strokes an expert player should need to complete the hole. The par for each hole is determined primarily by its length. For men, the USGA has set the following standards: under 250 yards, par 3; 251-470 yards, par 4; over 471 yards, par 5. Women's pars are: under 210 yards, par 3; 211-400 yards, par 4; 401-575 yards, par 5; over 576 yards, par 6. Most golf courses have a course par of about 72 strokes, which usually includes four par-3, four par-5, and 10 par-4 holes.

Playing a hole in two strokes less than par (earning a score of 3 on a par 5, for example) is referred to as an *eagle*, and playing one stroke under par is a *birdie*. A *bogey* is a score that is one stroke over par, and a *double-bogey* is two strokes over par.

On a typical 400-yard par-4 hole, a golfer might hit his driver about 225 yards, leaving 175 yards to the green. For his second shot, the golfer would choose an iron that he could hit that distance, such as a 5-iron. If the second shot landed a little short of the green, the golfer would use a pitching wedge to hit a high, short shot onto the green. From there, the golfer would attempt to putt the ball into the hole.

There are two types of golf competition: *stroke play* and *match play*. Professional tournaments, such as the Masters Championship or the British Open, follow the stroke play format. The golfer who records the lowest number of strokes during the tournament wins the competition.

Match play is scored hole by hole, and the winner is the player who has won the most holes during the round. If, during the round, a player has won three holes, his opponent has won one, and they have had the same score on, or split, the other holes, the player is said to be 2-up. The match is over when a player is ahead by more holes than the number remaining to be played. If a player is 2-up after the 17th hole, for example, he has won the match 2 and 1 (to play). The preliminary rounds of the U.S. Men's Amateur Championship are stroke play, but after the field is narrowed to 64 players, the final rounds follow the rules for match play.

GLOSSARY OF GOLF TERMS

—— ❦ ——

Ace: A hole in one.

Addressing the ball: When a player takes his stance and is preparing to hit the ball.

Approach: A stroke to the putting green; also, the section of fairway near the green.

Ball in play: A ball is in play as soon as the player has made a stroke on the teeing ground. It remains in play until holed out.

Birdie: A score of one stroke under par on a hole.

Bogey: A score of one stroke over par on a hole.

Bunker: A hazard in the fairway of a golf course consisting of an area of ground from which soil has been removed and replaced with soft sand.

Caddie: A person who carries a player's golf clubs, and often offers advice on how to play the course, during a round.

Chip: A short, low shot onto the green. A longer chip shot, which rolls toward the hole, is called a pitch-and-run.

Course: The whole area within which play is permitted.

Divot: A piece of turf uprooted by a club during a stroke. Golfers are usually urged to help maintain the course by replacing their divots when playing a round.

Double-bogey: A score of two strokes over par on a hole.

Eagle: A score that is two strokes under par for a hole.

Face: The part of a club that hits the ball.

Flagstick: A straight, moveable indicator, usually with a flag attached at the top, which is centered in the hole to show its position. The flag typically shows the number of the hole. The flagstick, which is also called the pin, is removed from the hole when players are attempting to putt.

"Fore!": A warning shout to anyone in the flight path of a ball.

Foursome: A group of four players.

Halved hole: In match play, a hole played in the same number of strokes by both players.

Handicap: The number of strokes over par it takes a player to complete an average round. For example, a player who usually shoots an 80 on a par-72 course would have an 8 handicap—eight strokes over par. Handicaps are set by USGA professionals and are based on the lowest 10 of a golfer's last 20 scores.

Hole: The hole, or cup, is the final target for the golfer. It is 4-1/2 inches in diameter and at least 4 inches deep. A player has holed out after a successful putt into the cup.

GLOSSARY

Honor: The side entitled to play first from the teeing ground is said to have the "honor." The player who recorded the lowest score on the previous hole has the honor on the next tee.

Hook: A shot that does not fly straight. A right-handed golfer's hook shot flies to the left, and a left-hander's hooks to the right. A *draw* is a controlled hook.

Lie: The position of a ball on the course.

Links: A seaside golf course. The most famous is the Old Course at St. Andrews Royal and Ancient Golf Course in Scotland.

Lost ball: A ball is lost if it is not found by the player after a five-minute search. There is a one-stroke penalty when a ball is lost.

Open: A tournament in which both professional and amateur players are allowed to compete.

Out of Bounds: Ground on which play is prohibited.

Par: The number of strokes an expert would need to complete a hole; also, the number of strokes required to play the entire course by an expert who makes no mistakes.

Penalty stroke: A stroke added to the score of a player, according to USGA rules. For example, if a ball is lost in a water hazard, the golfer plays another ball near the spot his first ball went into the water and takes a one-stroke penalty.

Pitch: A short approach shot in which the ball is lofted in a high arc onto the green.

Putt: A short stroke in which the ball rolls along the ground.

Putting green: The green is the area around the hole, which is specially prepared to allow the ball to roll easily.

Round: Playing the holes of the course in the correct order. Usually, a round is 18 holes.

Run: The distance a ball rolls after it hits the ground.

Slice: The opposite of a hook. A right-handed golfer's slice spins to the right side, and a left-hander's slice flies to the left. A *fade* is a controlled slice.

Stroke: Forward movement of the club made to move the ball.

Teeing ground: The starting place for the hole to be played.

Water hazard: Any lake, pond, river, ditch, or other open body of water on the golf course.

FURTHER READING

Durbin, Bill. *Tiger Woods* (Golf Legends). Philadelphia: Chelsea House Publishers, 1998.

Hull, Mary. *The Composite Guide to Golf*. Philadelphia: Chelsea House Publishers, 1998.

McCord, Gary, and John Huggan. *Golf for Dummies*. Foster City, Calif.: IDG Books Worldwide, 1995.

Nicklaus, Jack, and Ken Bowden. *Jack Nicklaus: My Story*. New York: Simon & Schuster, 1996.

Rosaforte, Tim. *Tiger Woods: The Makings of a Champion*. New York: St. Martin's Press, 1997.

Sports Illustrated staff. *Tiger Woods: The Making of a Champion*. New York: Fireside, 1997.

Strege, John. *Tiger: A Biography of Tiger Woods*. New York: Broadway, 1997.

Woods, Earl, and Pete McDaniel. *Training a Tiger*. New York: HarperCollins Publishers Inc., 1997.

INDEX

PICTURE CREDITS

2:   AP/Wide World Photos/ LM Otero

3:   AP/Wide World Photos/ Curtis Compton

10: AP/Wide World Photos/ Amy Sancetta

13: AP/Wide World Photos/ Dave Martin

14: AP/Wide World Photos/ Amy Sancetta

16-17: UPI/Corbis-Bettmann

18: AP/Wide World Photos/ Dave Martin

21: AP/Wide World Photos

23: AP/Wide World Photos/ Charles Dharapak

24: © Rick Dole/USGA

28: AP/Wide World Photos

31: photo courtesy Riviera Country Club

32: AP/Wide World Photos/ Ron Heflin

35: AP/Wide World Photos

36: AP/Wide World Photos/ Robin Loznak

39: AP/Wide World Photos

42: AP/Wide World Photos/ Curtis Compton

45: © Robert Walker/USGA

46: AP/Wide World Photos/ Charles Dharapak

48: AP/Wide World Photos/ Ron Heflin

50: UPI/Corbis-Bettmann

53: AP/Wide World Photos/ Dave Martin

56: AP/Wide World Photos/ Eric Gay

58: AP/Wide World Photos/ Lynne Sladky

60: AP/Wide World Photos/ Lynne Sladky

63: AP/Wide World Photos/ Matt York

65: AP/Wide World Photos/ Robin Loznak

68: AP/Wide World Photos/ Dave Martin

70: photo courtesy Department of Athletics, Stanford University

72: Courtesy Stanford University News Service

73: AP/Wide World Photos/ Susan Ragan

75: AP/Wide World Photos/ Phil Sandlin

78: AP/Wide World Photos/ Jack Atley-Melbourne

80: AP/Wide World Photos/ Jack Smith

82: AP/Wide World Photos/ Morry Gash

84: AP/Wide World Photos/ David Longstrath

86: AP/Wide World Photos/ Lennox McLendon

90: AP/Wide World Photos/ American Express

92: AP/Wide World Photos/ Mark Humphrey

93: AP/Wide World Photos/ Bill Waugh

95: AP/Wide World Photos/ Ron Heflin

98: AP/Wide World Photos/ Dave Martin

WILLIAM DURBIN is a graduate of the Bread Loaf School of English and has supervised writing research projects for the National Council of Teachers of English and Middlebury College. An avid writer and golfer, he teaches English at Cook High School in northeastern Minnesota and golf at Vermilion Fairways. His books include a young adult novel, *The Broken Blade*, and biographies of Arnold Palmer and Jack Nicklaus in Chelsea House Publishers' Legends of Golf series. A sequel to *The Broken Blade*, titled *Wintering*, is expected in 1998.

NATHAN IRVIN HUGGINS, one of America's leading scholars in the field of black studies, helped select the titles for the BLACK AMERICANS OF ACHIEVEMENT series, for which he also served as senior consulting editor. He was the W. E. B. Du Bois Professor of History and Afro-American Studies at Harvard University and the director of the W. E. B. Du Bois Institute for Afro-American Research at Harvard. He received his doctorate from Harvard in 1962 and returned there as professor in 1980 after teaching at Columbia University, the University of Massachusetts, Lake Forest College, and the California State University, Long Beach. He was the author of four books and dozens of articles, including *Black Odyssey: The Afro-American Ordeal in Slavery*, *The Harlem Renaissance*, and *Slave and Citizen: The Life of Frederick Douglass*, and was associated with the Children's Television Workshop, National Public Radio, the Boston Athenaeum, the Museum of Afro-American History, the Howard Thurman Educational Trust, and Upward Bound. Professor Huggins died in 1989, at the age of 62, in Cambridge, Massachusetts.